# 10 LEPERS

# 10 LEPERS

## a bible study
### michael e. loomis

## AMBASSADOR INTERNATIONAL
#### GREENVILLE, SOUTH CAROLINA & BELFAST, NORTHERN IRELAND

www.ambassador-international.com

# 10 LEPERS
*A Bible Study*

Printed in the United States of America

ISBN: 978-1-62020-100-8
eISBN: 978-1-62020-150-3

Unless otherwise indicated,
Scripture is from the King James Version.

Cover Design by Justin Hall
Page Layout by Justin Hall

AMBASSADOR INTERNATIONAL
Emerald House
427 Wade Hampton Blvd.
Greenville, SC 29609, USA
www.ambassador-international.com

AMBASSADOR BOOKS
The Mount
2 Woodstock Link
Belfast, BT6 8DD, Northern Ireland, UK
www.ambassador-international.com

*The colophon is a trademark of Ambassador*

*In memory of Sam Centioli:*

*The first man to whom I publicly confirmed*

*my faith in Jesus Christ.*

*He became a friend and mentor*

*who too soon was called home*

*to be with the Lord.*

# CHAP TERS

# PREFACE

Leprosy is a terrible and disfiguring disease. Numb to the touch, patches of red and scaly skin alert the unaware sufferer that something serious is occurring within his or her own body. The unknown malady does not respond to any medicine that they may have on hand. Instead, more numb red patches and sores are noticed on other parts of the body. And, in fact, the Leprosy may have been growing in their body for years. When the skin condition can no longer be covered by clothing and is no longer hidden, it is noticed by family members or friends, thus raising questions that embarrass the sufferer. When the disease is diagnosed, the infected person is avoided, ostracized by all those who once cared for the individual. All these family members know is that it is highly infectious and they don't want it to spread to them or their other loved ones. The individual is forced out of their home and job.

The disease conjures the image of pain caused by rotting and infected body parts that soon fall away from the body. The inexperienced on-looker believes the fingers and toes of the sufferer will eventually fall off. The nose will fall away or will become severely misshapen. Sexual dysfunction will occur, particularly for the male. Blindness will come soon. Legs and hands will become deformed, making coordination and walking in any normal way impossible. Any minor cut or abrasion will not be repaired well by the body, causing abscesses and infection.

Because the body cannot repair itself, one is sick and experiencing pain throughout the body.

Because of their ejection from home and hearth, shelter becomes a high priority that is not normally met well. They will now suffer from the elements of the weather. Because they are ostracized, their clothing will wear thin and will cause them more extensive exposure to the elements. Because they have no more support structure, or a very minimal one, they are not receiving the sustenance or nutrition necessary for them to keep the health they have, though degrading with the disease. Their downward slide to even poorer health progresses more quickly. Because they have no support structure, the sufferer is forced to beg, borrow, and steal the necessities of life, at least as long as they have the mobility to do so. The disease, at least historically, creates a downward spiral that can only end in death.

Even today, the progression of the disease of Leprosy can only be halted, not cured. Any ravages caused by the disease up to the point of arrest cannot be corrected. As a result, the patches of numbness, the decreased organ functions, and its crippling effects cannot be reversed.

This book, The Ten Lepers, takes a Biblical view of Leprosy and equates the destruction of the physical disease with the spiritual destruction caused by sin in the heart of mankind. But, in contrast to the physical disease of Leprosy, in the spiritual realm there is a cure for "Spiritual Leprosy." And, in truth, the effects of spiritual Leprosy cannot only be cured, they can be reversed. It is my prayer that you will read this book, along with God's Word, and will accept the free cure supplied by Jesus Christ and will then work toward the goal of ridding your life of the effects of a disease-ridden life caused by your spiritual Leprosy.

# 1: A WICKED DISEASE

Personally, I don't really remember ever having heard the nuns say that Father Damien's fingers and nose had fallen off. I do, though, remember my fellow Catholic school classmates telling me that leprosy causes one's fingers, nose, and feet to fall off. Were they kidding me? This didn't really happen with leprosy, right? All I know is that leprosy scared me silly!

Here was Father Damien, born Jozef De Veuster in Tremelo, Belgium[1], volunteering to go to some deserted tropical island. Relegated to a leper colony on a small beach where food and supplies came only from small boats or from donkeys led over the mountain pass, he chooses to go and live with lepers in what clearly becomes a life sentence when he becomes infected with the disease.

He's living on an island that's hot, rainy, and muggy. He can't grow crops. People from the main Hawaiian Islands can't easily supply him and his leper colony regularly. But, the man becomes a leader. He, with the help of his leprous friends, builds St. Philomena, the leper colony's church. They build houses for the colony's inhabitants. Molokai, his island, is never the same. Today it is remembered as a place where Fr. Damien took a stand to help others and became a legend and example of how a man can devote his life to serving his fellow man. In the end, it gave me hope that man may not be so bad after all.

Years later, I now see pictures of Fr. Damien in his last days. It doesn't look like his nose or fingers are missing, though the write-ups that accompany this picture indicate that he is in the final stages of leprosy and is near death.[2] The facts indicate that he was quite sick. One leg was dragging as he walked. One foot was in bandages. An arm was in a sling. He ended his days in a flurry of building activities so that his family of lepers could have more houses in which to live before he, himself, died. As a child, I stood in fear and awe of this man who put himself through so much to serve others. I wanted to be like him but knew that I did not have the courage to follow his path.

My generation probably remembers seeing the movie or reading the touching story of Ben Hur, a Tale of the Christ.[3]  Ben Hur, a Jewish aristocrat who lives in Jerusalem, is persecuted and sent to row and die in the Roman galleys by the Roman tribune, Messala, who was his boyhood friend. Through an exciting and intricate story plot, Ben Hur is freed and is driven to seek out and find his mother and sister, also imprisoned by Messala.

When Messala's aide finds them in the Roman dungeons, they are found to be leprous and are released from prison to avoid contaminating others. By and by, they leave the city only to be, again, relegated to life and death with other lepers outside the city where they live in the caves that weave beneath the city. They have no hope, are sickly, and are near death. As the story goes, but for this son and brother and Jesus Christ, they would have died the ignominious life of a leper: shamed, dishonored, despicable, untouchable, and disgraced. They are cured miraculously, the only known way to be cured of leprosy during that time period. It isn't a true story, but it's indicative of how lepers have been treated throughout the ages.

Today, I look at leprosy and know that it has been addressed by the medical research community, but this "address" has only been done within the last one hundred years. While a full cure has not yet been discovered, the disease has been arrested so that those who suffer from the disease may return to society after receiving short, effective treatments of antibiotics followed by a life-long medicinal regimen that affords the person a normal life. I thank the Lord for such work and treatment. Clearly, this type of successful medical work has not always been able to be done by man. Thus, leprosy has been a devastating illness for millennia.

Before this recent one hundred years, those with leprosy were forced to hide their disease for as long as possible. It was their terrible secret. Until "found out," they would live a life of lies, hoping that no one discovered their horrible illness. When discovered by those around them—possibly when someone else noticed that the sufferer was experiencing no pain in an area that had been burned, cut, or injured in some way—the leper was taken away in order to prevent leprosy from spreading to others. Their worst fears were well founded.

With no cure, they were most certainly banished from family, friends, and society for life. Likely, they were removed from a life that had been at least somewhat comfortable, having had the companionship of friends and family, clothing, shelter, and food. Wherever they were sent, they were assuredly going to be poor. No one would want to touch them, and, therefore, no one would touch any type of product that they made if it was known to be made by a leper's hands. Sure, family might be able to get food to them, but would that last? Would their families continue to support them for a lifetime or—more specifically—for their own lifetime? This kind of hope was too much to dream of for them. Thus, their life became one of severe poverty. They had no reason to expect anything better.

The disease of leprosy has much to teach today's men and women. From a biblical perspective, leprosy speaks to us about sin. This sin is infectious, drawing its victims further and further from productive lives. It separates us from that which is good, service to our Lord Jesus

Christ, our families, and those with whom we come into contact during our daily walk through life. Then, not only does the person who does not believe on Jesus Christ remain infected with the horrible leprous condition of this one "sin," this man or woman is weakened further yet, becoming infected with other  maladies that cause life to become even more dysfunctional and sinful. This may sound a bit confusing to the reader now, but it can be readily explained with the following example.

The leper for our example may be a drug addict. To support his habit, he may need to steal from family and friends, thus becoming a thief. Later, he may be pulled into selling the drugs he's using, becoming a drug dealer. The crowd he "runs with" may also like alcohol, tempting him to start using alcohol in addition to his drugs; now he becomes an alcoholic in addition to everything else. One can easily add to the list of maladies that now infect the leper, though they are not specifically his "leprous condition," only sins that have been added to the list. It's clear that the person is not serving Jesus Christ. He is not even serving a society that is not God-fearing. He's serving himself. Unless his leprosy is turned around or cured, his sin will cause a separation from Jesus Christ that is an eternal one.

In this study, a biblical study, we will look at several ways that leprosy affected the sufferer both physically and spiritually. Then, we'll determine how we can treat the "spiritual sin" disease of leprosy.

# 2: A PHYSICAL DISEASE

Leprosy is one of those sneaky diseases. Long before you know you're infected, it's incubating and slowly developing in your body. Some say that leprosy can hide in your system for up to thirty years[4] before it manifests itself in some visible manner. Normally, though, it shows itself in anywhere from five to fifteen years.[5] The point is that this disease takes up residence in an individual's body without any indication that it is there. Maybe it will lie dormant, awaiting the right circumstances in which to awaken and grow until it is noticed by its host or by others. Maybe the individual becomes infected and starts a slow progression that can last for years, with nerves tingling or degrading, causing spots on the skin to grow numb for seemingly no reason. Regardless of the original date of infection, it is growing in the victim's body. Whatever damage that it does is permanent and irreversible, although its progress can now be stopped with antibiotics and other medicines.

How does it enter the victim's system? Mucous or saliva from a leprosy sufferer, who may not even know that he or she has it, can carry the bacteria and be transferred to other individuals who have come into contact with the sufferer—the donor. Contact from the leprous donor may be via liquid, actual saliva or mucous, or in vapor form, possibly from a sneeze or simply by "breathing too closely," and is thus breathed in by the new host. It takes so long to see symptoms of the disease that the new sufferer—the new host—is unaware of how or from whom the disease was spread.

Mostly, the disease seems to be spread by people in developing countries. The more common ages for seeing the actual outbreak of the infection is in people who are in their twenties and thirties, but it has been experienced by young and old alike. Additionally, the disease is known to be resident in dirt, armadillos, and possibly even mosquitoes and bedbugs, though as yet unproven. The good news is that most experts agree that ninety-five percent of the population is immune to the infection—or at least their immune systems fight the disease off when a possible receiver has come into contact with a donor. Seemingly, one does not need to worry too much about becoming infected with the disease. Ah, but the problem is whether you are in the ninety-five percent or the five percent. In essence, newer medical research indicates that there is a defect in cell-mediated immunity within the victim that causes the susceptibility to the leprosy bacteria. One might say that they were born to get leprosy once some sort of sustained or serious exposure occurs.

Initial affected locations are the skin and the nerves. It has even been reported by some that one of the first signs of leprosy is that the eyelashes and eyebrows fall out.[6] Rashes and bumps are seen on the skin. Bumps can enlarge to the degree that the face is disfigured. This disfigurement brings about the term that was quite common around the time of Jesus Christ when leprosy was known as "elephantiasis" (though it may not truly have been leprosy that was noted). Nerves become deadened, resulting in weakening muscles and areas on the skin that are insensitive to touch or changes in temperature. This, it is speculated, is where the idea that fingers, toes, noses, and even hands and feet fall off of leprosy victims. The disease does not actually cause the "amputation." Instead, when a victim's skin is burned or scratched, the skin does not "report" the actual damage to the body's nervous system. Therein lies the problem. The body does not pick up its cues from the damaged body part to start the healing process. The body member starts to infect and decay, resulting in the finger or toe shrinking or rotting away from the body.

When the muscles become weakened, the body's movements and coordination change. Flopping foot, or "footdrop," starts to become a visible part of the disease's effect on the sufferer due to muscles that have become too weak to carry the load. When nerves no longer receive messages from or send messages to the brain, muscles no longer contract or stretch properly. The hand's grip becomes clumsy and uncontrolled. With the now-unresponsive hand muscles, the hand can deform into a "claw." Swelling occurs both in the muscles and the nerves. They swell enough that a doctor can feel the increase in size of the nerves and muscles when examining the patient. Not surprisingly, the sufferer undergoes serious pain throughout all of these manifestations of the disease.

Leprosy progresses and starts to affect other parts of the body too. The feet may develop sores or ulcers, making it painful to walk. The nasal passages become damaged—and eroded if untreated—and create a chronically stuffy nose. The nose actually collapses and deforms at these advanced stages. Nosebleeds may also occur at this point. Damage to the eyes occurs, leading to glaucoma and eventually to blindness. For the male, sexual dysfunction occurs, causing genital shrinkage, infertility, and impotence. Untreated leprosy causes additional nerve damage, problems with the lymph nodes and the immune system, kidney problems that result in kidney failure, and liver damage. These can lead to the death of the leprosy victim. Death doesn't really come specifically from leprosy in the sense that leprosy is "the killer" of its host. Instead, leprosy causes many conditions that create a domino effect. Nerve damage results in accidental damage to skin and finally degradation of these organs which can result in infections and death—again, only if the condition goes untreated.

There are three main types of leprosy: tuberculoid, lepromatus, and borderline. For our purposes, these three variations simply apply to the severity of the conditions that the sufferer will undergo and the prognosis for their individual treatments. Of the three, lepromatus, or Mycobacterium Lepromatosis, is the most severe. If untreated, it can be lethal due to its final stages of nerve damage. These main forms of leprosy have been termed "Hansen's Disease" because, in 1873, G. H. Armauer Hansen effectively isolated and classified the main types of leprosy: the "causative agents." Once isolated, the door was opened for future scientists to understand leprosy and to develop treatments for the disease.

Later in this book, we will simply discuss leprosy in a generic fashion so that the reader need not worry about being overwhelmed by more medical terminology. All forms of leprosy show signs of the condition on the skin in the form of rashes of various colors and bumps, along with the numbing or the insensitivity of the skin as the disease progresses. In effect, the leprosy sufferer would qualify as "unclean," regardless of the variation of leprosy he or she had, as you will see from the biblical accounts in this book. All forms can lead to serious consequences and death when untreated.

The history of leprosy is varied, as are its treatments. Known as elephantiasis in the ancient Greek world, treatments varied from the patient being fed animals' blood, such as from dogs and lambs, and even to being given blood from human corpses. Later, venom of bees, cobras, frogs, and scorpions all were used in attempts to cure leprosy victims. Chemicals such as arsenic, creosote, salt, and oils—one called "Chalmoogra Oil"—were used, again with limited success and essentially no real cures. Only in the middle of the twentieth century would serious medicines such as rifampicin, clofazimine, and dapsone truly arrest the progress of the disease within the sufferer.

Leprosy has been detected in bodily remains that are 4,000 years old in India.[7] This reinforces the prevalence of the disease and verifies that leprosy truly was a factor with which to be contended for eras of time that pre-date the recorded history of man. An account has been found where an Indian surgeon named Sushrata wrote about leprosy around 600 BC, though his writings were not discovered until the fourth century AD.

As far as secular history is recorded, leprosy was actually written about and described accurately around the time of Jesus Christ. Aulus Cornelius Celsus, a Roman recording accounts of the disease in his book "De Medicina," wrote about leprosy as "elephantiasis" in about the year 25 BC up through about the year 37 AD. Pliny the Elder, another Roman, wrote about the disease in the 23 to 79 AD time frame. Galen of Pergamum gave one of the more accurate descriptions of leprosy in 150 AD.

The disease was recorded in Persia (modern-day Iran) during the Middle Ages by a man named Avicenna. Leprosy is also noted in Europe during the Middle Ages. Matthew Paris, a Benedictine Monk from that time period, stated that there were approximately 19,000 cases of leprosy in Europe in the 1200s (AD). Incidentally, this time period reveals the first occurrences of leper colonies and demonstrates that separation, whether forced or voluntary, of lepers from society continued to be practiced. The idea that lepers were cursed and sinful remains a base assumption for the view that they contracted the disease in the first place during this medieval era.

China and Japan show significant numbers of accounts and descriptions of leprosy from this medieval age through today. All of the standard symptoms for leprosy are described there. Additionally, the standard methods of isolation and attempted treatments are noted in Japan.

Even in the United States of America, leprosy has been of great concern. In 1921, a leprosy disease center called Gillis W. Long Hansen's Disease Center was established in Carville, Louisiana.[8] Used for two purposes, a live-in treatment center and a place for research, Carville became notable as a place where effective drugs for the treatment of leprosy were developed.

It may be noted at this point that early diagnoses of leprosy in ancient times may or may not have been leprosy. Though many may have been the actual disease of leprosy, they may be accounts of syphilis,[9] eczema, psoriasis,[10] lupus, ringworm, and favus (an infectious skin fungus).[11] Without the modern analytical medical systems that we have today, these illnesses may have been assumed to be the disease of leprosy. To many people in ancient and even medieval days, a skin rash was a sign that the individual must have contracted leprosy. They truly had no way to differentiate specific illnesses and were forced, for the protection of their own society, into calling it leprosy and isolating those perceived to be victims of it. Later, if the skin condition cleared up—in that it was no longer seen on the skin—the individual could be "certified" clean and returned to society. So, though we will be talking about leprosy as seen in the Bible, it is true that some leprosy sufferers may have only had a case of psoriasis or eczema. To the man of that day, it looked like leprosy.

Throughout the centuries, individuals of note who have contracted leprosy are recorded in many accounts. We have already discussed the Roman Catholic priest on Molokai, Jozef De Veuster (a.k.a. Fr. Damien), and many others can be added to the list. In Jerusalem during the Crusades, Baldwin IV, king in the Latin portion of Jerusalem (as depicted in the movie The Kingdom of Heaven[12]), was dying severely disfigured by leprosy. Japan adds a feudal lord to the list, a man named Otani Yoshitsugu. Vietnam adds a poet named Han Mac Tu. For the purposes of this book, though, biblical figures who had or were given leprosy will be the focus. Many Old Testament biblical figures such as Moses' sister Miriam, Naaman the Syrian commander, Elisha's servant Gehazi, as well as New Testament figures will be discussed in brief as this book progresses. The main account that we will study will be the healing of the ten lepers in the Gospel of Luke.

# 3: A SPIRITUAL DISEASE

L eprosy, biblically speaking, is not only sneaky with its capability of bodily destruction, but it is also viewed as blackest sin in the Scriptures. This sounds pretty harsh. Here is a person who has no idea where he or she caught the disease and has no idea whether it will ever go away. God in His Word uses the disease to show that an infected person is to live afar off to prevent its spread into surrounding communities. In the Scriptures, leprosy reflects the spiritual side of man's nature in the sin that is deep down inside every person on earth. Let's take a deeper look at the leper and this scriptural view.

Old Testament discussions and accounts of leprosy set the tone for this scriptural view in both the Old and New Testaments. In the Old Testament, two words are used to relate the illness of leprosy to the reader. The first word is tsara,[13] a Hebrew word with its root meaning having the idea of scourging. Here, the thought is that leprosy is a severe punishment that includes personal suffering. The one who has leprosy is being punished or is given some serious trouble and affliction. In other words, the Old Testament looks at the individual sufferer as having been "stricken with leprosy." So, when one reads the word "leprosy" in the Old Testament, it is relating the idea of being stricken with leprosy.[14] It means that one is a leper or is leprous; one has leprosy.

The second Hebrew word used in the Old Testament for leprosy is tsaraath.[15] Clearly, the root word here is from tsara. It simply means leprosy and refers to a fungus and mold more than the human disease.[16]

For our purposes, the concept that we will use from within the Old Testament is that leprosy is viewed as the result of mankind's sinfulness. It doesn't always mean that someone has done something specific to earn the affliction but more so that man is sinful in his base nature. Man is born in sin. Psalm 51:5 reveals that David saw himself as a sinner even from the point of conception. Was the act of conception a sin for David's mother and father? No. Hebrews 13:4 states for us that the marriage bed is pure and undefiled. The act of procreation within marriage is not a sin. Scripture does make it very clear that we are sinful and that we are so even from our earliest moments in life. Jeremiah 17:9 says that our hearts are deceitful above all things and are desperately wicked. No one can know the human heart because it is so black. Our hearts generate all sorts of sinful thoughts and acts. Out of man's heart proceeds evil thoughts, murders, adulteries, fornications, thefts, false witness, and blasphemies; these things that come out of a man make the man sinful (Matthew 15:19-20). Said in short, we have no right to blame others for our sinful failures.

Nothing man seems to do from within his root nature does any good or produces true righteousness. The Prophet Micah stated that the good man had perished from the face of the earth (Micah 7:2-4). Those who remained were awaiting the opportunity to go after other men's blood, hunting every man. They were doing evil and were pursuing mischievous desires. Even the most upright man was no good in Micah's view, being no more than a thorny briar. He knew one thing, though. The day would come when these evil men would receive their comeuppance (Micah 7:4).

The Prophet Isaiah said it another way. We may think we're good and are doing righteous (i.e., "good") things. But in Isaiah 64:6, he tells the human race that they are unclean and that their "doing good" doesn't count for anything in God's eyes. Their "righteousness" is as filthy rags to God. Not only that, we are not here very long. Our lives will fade like the life of a leaf. It flutters in the wind, soaks in the sun, and stands for nothing. It is easily killed by the cool air of fall. Like the dead leaf or the leaf torn from the tree, we will allow sin to carry us away in life, taking us away from the lives that God would have us live. But, there's no reason to feel disheartened. God has made beautiful plans for those who have faith in Him (Isaiah 64:4). All we need to do is look to Him for salvation (Isaiah 64:5).

In the meantime, let me reinforce the view that leprosy is a result of the sinful nature of man. We know, after developing a clearer physical view on the nature of leprosy in chapter 2, that leprosy is nothing but a bacteria that is contagious to five percent of the earth's population. But, the Bible is stating that "spiritual leprosy" is representative of man's sinful nature, a nature that grows more corrupt throughout a man's life unless a cure is found.

The New Testament shows the leper as an outcast, a person who needs to be cured and then sent to the priest to be verified clean and cured (Luke 5:14 and 17:14). This methodology comes from the treatment of leprosy in the Old Testament in Leviticus, chapter 14. Thus, the leper of Jesus' day is treated in an Old Testament fashion and is held in the Old Testament view: that of being a person who has been punished due to sin.

The wording used in the New Testament is similar in nature to that of the Old Testament but isn't used in the sense of leprosy being a "scourging" of the individual. The idea that it is a punishment, though, does carry over from the Old Testament priestly handling of the leper and the isolation of the leper from society with all of the procedures that must be followed.

Leviticus chapter 13 goes into great detail regarding the analysis of skin problems that may or not be leprosy. The Levitical priest is directed to take great time and care in the determination of that which is leprosy and that which isn't. When leprosy has been confirmed, the leper is called "unclean" and is forced to wear clothes in a certain way, covering his face with a cloth, wearing no covering on his head, and dwelling alone outside the community or camp. Being a defiled person, the sufferer is now clearly seen by anyone within eyesight as a leper. Everywhere they went, they were forced to call out "unclean" to all those whom they came near. This is the view of the leper during the time of Jesus Christ.

In the New Testament, the word lepis describes a condition where the skin is flaking or scaling and peels off. Actually, it can apply to the scales on a fish and is also the word used to describe the scales that fell from Saul's (Paul's) eyes after his encounter with Jesus Christ on the road to Damascus (Acts 9:18). So, the word can be used minimally as a reference to leprosy. One carries it a bit too far when using it as the term of leprosy in detail.[17] The only thing to remember here is that it is the root of the word leprosy.

The word lepra refers to a variety of skin disorders that include leprosy.[18] As previously shown, it can be Hansen's disease of leprosy, but also includes many types of rashes, psoriasis, lupus, ringworm, and the like. The problem is that the people of Jesus' day did not have the ability to make a more accurate diagnosis of the specific disease the sufferer was experiencing. To the first century priest or doctor, the disease was leprosy. If at some point the disease went away, its disappearance was either a cure from God, or it had simply been a more minor skin ailment that finally healed. They were looking at a skin disease and had to treat it in accordance with their directives as put forth in Leviticus chapters 13 and 14. Actually, this view—that leprosy may have been a mixture of diseases and skin problems—will help accentuate the problems of sin with mankind later on in this study.

The specific term for leprosy in the New Testament is lepros and again refers to a serious skin disease or disorder. This is the word used in the account we will study regarding the healing of the ten lepers, and it is directly used in Luke 17:12.[19]

As we start studying the healing of the ten lepers, we need to understand a few things about the setting in which Jesus Christ healed these men. Luke is the writer, in the power of the Holy Spirit, of this Gospel. Luke is a physician and is a dear friend of Paul, the apostle to the Gentiles (Colossians 4:14). Being a physician or medical doctor, Luke's descriptions regarding cures and healings tend to be more clinical and say much for his care in writing portions that have to do with such in his Gospel account and in the account he writes of the early church's growth and travels: the Acts of the Apostles (Luke 1:3-4, Acts 1:1). Luke seems to take extra care in writing the Gospel account as if he is writing it to the Gentile world rather than Jewish. It's quite likely that Luke was a Gentile, or at least he was a Jew raised in an environment that was not near Jerusalem, the hub of Jewish life, rituals, and law.[20] Because of his writing and profession, he writes very well in Greek and does not seem to know Aramaic, the language that Jesus Christ was most likely to have spoken from His childhood. The reason for singling Luke out as a Gentile seems to be corroborated in Colossians 4:10-14. Paul sends the greetings of Aristarchus, Marcus, and Justus as three fellow workers of the circumcision (Colossians 4:10-11). Being circumcised, they are Jews. Separately, he sends the greetings of Epaphras, Demas, and Luke in verses 12 through 14, dividing them out of the group of circumcised Jews. Again, Luke is most likely a Gentile physician. For our study, it's good to keep in mind that Luke's writings seem to convey his desire to win the Gentile world to Christ. He, being a Gentile, is an outsider looking into a faith that has given hope to not only the Jews but also the remainder of the world—the Gentiles. He wants to see Gentiles saved and gives pertinent information within this Gospel to make them feel invited into salvation through our Lord Jesus Christ.

As for the time period, Jesus is in His third year of ministry and is soon to be crucified. The Pharisees would be sending out spies to catch Him and turn Him in, as seen in Luke 20:20, and they would plot to betray and kill Him in Luke 22:2, 4. Judas would betray Him with a kiss in the garden (Luke 22:47-48). This all happened but a few days after the healing of the ten lepers. Jesus is under a sense of urgency where He wants to win the world to Him, but the Jews have now clearly denied His deity and work, rejecting Him totally by having Him crucified.

The political climate is tense. The Jews hate their Roman overlords, but they must answer to their capturing kings who are placed into power over them: people like Herod, Pilate, and Caesar (Luke 23). The Pharisees and priests used the system well, though, requiring that Pilate crucify Jesus Christ (Luke 23:23). Their rejection of Jesus Christ would prove to be their undoing, as Jerusalem and all Judea would finally be crushed by the Romans and their temple leveled in 70 AD.[21] Though the Jewish leaders hated the Romans, they linked with them to put Jesus to death. They linked themselves to a world governmental system in order to keep their business of religion, their lone hold of the way to heaven in the world. They do not want to give their seemingly sole right to redemption away to the rest of the world but rather want to be able to sell their religion to those who are willing and able to pay for it. They seem to say, "Heaven knows we don't want to sully heaven with the poor, maimed, and afflicted. Let's keep it for ourselves: the Pharisees, scribes, Levites, and so on. If we force God into a corner, He will have to do things the way in which we desire they be done." They are wrong. God is neither to be mocked nor placed into our small, frail views or boxes of what He should be as a God in our eyes (Galatians 6:3, 7), but He will eternally be the God to whom we answer for the work done in this life (Hebrews 6:1-3).

Interestingly enough, Luke is the only Gospel writer to include this passage on the ten lepers in his account of Christ's walk on earth. Luke writes of several miracles that Jesus performed that are only accounted for in the Gospel of Luke. This study is unique and powerful and affords the reader a glimpse into Christ's heart for the lost, both Jew and Gentile.

Now, let's look at the passage of the healing of the ten lepers:

## LUKE 17:11-19

*And it came to pass, as he went to Jerusalem, that he passed through the midst of Samaria and Galilee. And as he entered into a certain village, there met him ten men that were lepers, which stood afar off: And they lifted up their voices, and said, Jesus, Master, have mercy on us. And when he saw them, he said unto them, Go shew yourselves unto the priests. And it came to pass, that, as they went, they were cleansed. And one of them, when he saw that he was healed, turned back, and with a loud voice glorified God, And fell down on his face at his feet, giving him thanks: and he was a Samaritan. And Jesus answering said, Were there not ten cleansed? but where are the nine? There are not found that returned to give glory to God, save this stranger. And he said unto him, Arise, go thy way: thy faith hath made thee whole.*

## LUKE 17:11-19
*Verse 11*

Jesus knows His own path. He knows that this walk to Jerusalem will be His last before He endures persecution and crucifixion (Luke 18: 31-33). He knows that He must finish that which was prophesied by the Old Testament prophets. He will be delivered (i.e., betrayed), beaten, mocked, spit upon, and scourged (in other words, "whipped"), and then He will be put to death. All of this will be to His greater glory as He rises on the third day after His crucifixion with an eternal and glorified body. Though He knows all of these things and how hard it will be physically for Him to accept and undergo them, He proceeds undaunted. He continues His work, even as the reality of His pending and humiliating death is clearly on His mind. It is necessary for us to realize that He did not have to choose this method of saving mankind, but He submitted to the shame and pain of the cross in order to accomplish man's salvation and to again sit down at His Father's right hand. He was fulfilling His Father's will (Matthew 26:39, 42, John 8:29). As I read this, I understand how hard it would be to submit like Jesus did. Would we do for Him as He did for us? I do not believe that many today would have the strength to press on to the goal if we knew the way in which we would die. But, again, here Jesus is walking with single-minded determination toward Jerusalem, and He provides healing and solace to others as He makes the trip.

## LUKE 17:11-19
*Verse 12*

These ten lepers were following the directive laid down in Leviticus 13 to "stand afar off." They were not scattered in the crowd, and they didn't force their way closer to Jesus to speak with Him face to face. It would have been clear to the crowd watching them that they were lepers simply by their mode of dress. Their garments would have been dark in color, covered them from head to toe, and would mostly have been tattered rags. Their faces, from the nose down over the beard, would have been covered. Standing ten men in a group, they would have given the crowd a wide berth, and the crowd would have kept their distance with no problem. No one wanted to catch this supposedly highly contagious disease. No one wanted to join their ranks of uncleanness, poverty, and social ostracism. The crowd would have been terrified if they had gotten too close to them. Prior to seeing Jesus, they would have been calling out to the crowd, "Unclean, Unclean!" in order to announce their leprous presence. This all was directed by the law in Leviticus (13:45, 46).

Wherever Jesus travelled, people knew who He was and what He was doing within His ministry to mankind. They knew how He could heal without even a touch. They knew His power. His reputation as a compassionate man and healer preceded Him. No one who had ever approached him for salvation or healing, or both, was ever turned away. Though the town is not mentioned, these lepers knew who He was. This group of ten socially unclean rejects knew what they were doing. They were on a mission to meet Jesus. Had they travelled far? It doesn't seem likely, given that they appear to know the area and, when Jesus told them to go and see the priests, they had no questions about the location but went immediately on their way.

Really, it does not matter what city, county, town, state, country, or region that these lepers were in. It didn't matter where Jesus was. Wherever we are, we can meet Jesus. He is always wherever we need to be. All we need to do is seek after Him, for He has already come to our location and is in our presence.

Think about this group of lepers. They were ten men. We can be sure that the background of each man was varied in as much as each one was an individual in life. Some would have come from poor backgrounds, and some would have been wealthy in their previous life as standard citizens of the realm. Now, their backgrounds no longer mattered. They were all poor and ostracized in their disease. Their worldly wealth, or prior lack of it, mattered little at this moment in time. They had nothing but the clothes on their backs. As previously discussed, even the food that would sustain them was limited and rare in coming—if those relatives and friends who had previously known and loved them were not able or willing to get supplies to them. As a group, it's quite likely that they were hungry. Their families, including all wives, sons, daughters, fathers, mothers, relatives, and such, had been placed in the position of ejecting them from their homes when the sinful scourge was found in them.

We must realize that they were all individuals. Each man had a calling and work that had to be left behind. They might have been farmers, tax collectors, business managers, or beggars. No details are given. For us, we could picture them as engineers, technicians, plant managers, salesmen, craftsmen, meat cutters, business owners, clerks, and the like. In the world of lepers, all were now equal. They were sick, jobless, homeless, hungry, and poor.

Is it really any different today? As we succumb to addictions, are we not completely submitted to them? Whether it be alcohol, drugs, sex, pornography, money, leisure, cigarettes, or whatever kind of self-driven lust that we set our minds to, we have moved from being a useful member of society to being a self-centered individual who has given up his previously useful life and has become a poor useless weight upon society, shirking his duties and serving only himself. Is this harsh? Yes, but one must realize that this is how leprosy has been viewed too. Society had ostracized these people, not only thinking of them as unclean, but believing them to be unclean because of their sinful lifestyles.

The book of Romans puts it this way. We are servants of these lusts and items of greed if we allow them to become our gods in life

(Romans 6:16). Leprosy, as a spiritual representation of sin, indicates the depravity into which we submit ourselves when we become totally debauched in these sins and addictions. We withdraw from society. We are useless to society. We become scavengers to fulfill our own personal needs. Family and friends can no longer rely on us. In fact, family and friends may no longer want anything to do with us and may choose to stop all support, allowing us to wallow and die in the addiction we've chosen over them. Like it or not, the spiritual leper must realize that this is tough love. If the leper (i.e., addict) is completely submitted to his or her own greed and lusts, there is, in the end, nothing a family member or friend can do for that one but to abandon him to his own desires and personal drives even though those things lead to death. All family and friends can pray for is the healing that one needs from God.

As fingers and nose become disfigured, and as feet become swollen, ulcerated, and crippled, the leper is an apt example of the self-serving addict or person who is completely ensconced in his own sin as job, family, respectability, and capabilities fall away. He has become unable to serve anyone else, or even to support his own family, having crippled himself in his slavery to sin: his addiction. He has abandoned his duties only to become abandoned by God who allows him to take the path he has chosen (Romans 1:28-31). Regardless of our chosen sin, God will let us serve our own selves if we totally turn from Him and reject His offer of salvation.

## LUKE 17:11-19
*Verse 13*

Can you hear the lepers lifting their voices up to Jesus? It would not have been a casual call. Desperation would have colored the cry of ten voices as they called out with sincerity and energy. They were making their group's plea at loud volume! They were not going to let

the opportunity of meeting Jesus pass by but would get His attention in order to receive His word of healing. At this point in time, the
crowd would have melted into the background. The lepers may not
have been directly "in His face" but would have now been standing in
their own space in His presence. They had succeeded in getting the
attention of Jesus Christ.

These ten outcasts were calling Jesus their Master. They were in
effect accepting Him as their commander and were giving Him direct
power over their lives. This was a rare time or example in the New
Testament where anyone but Jesus' disciples called Him Master. These
men were placing Him in charge of their lives. They knew that only
God could heal leprosy, as stated in the Leviticus 14 passage. Thus,
they knew that Jesus must be God in the form of man upon the earth.
They were not going to allow Jesus to pass by them without commu-
nicating with Him.

The interesting thing about the statement that comes from the lips
of these ten men is that it is not a specific request for healing. It is a
request for mercy, reinforcing the fact that they viewed their leprosy
as being a scourge or judgment from God. They believed that God
was "whipping them" because of their sins. Clearly, they knew that
they needed mercy, the Greek word eleeo, meaning that they wanted
His compassion and pity. They were asking for His forgiveness as an
act of compassion to them. Figuratively, at least, they were on their
knees before Him, recognizing that He was the only solution to their
problems in life.

## LUKE 17:11-19

*Verse 14*

Jesus handled their request in a very interesting manner. He didn't
carry on a conversation with them. They asked no further favors of
Him. This verse states simply that He saw them and told them to go

and show themselves to the priests. He doesn't state that they have or will be cleansed, or healed, of their leprosy. His only directive is that they are to "go" to the priests and "show." They had already placed their faith in Him when they called Him "Master." Now, He was making them put feet to their faith. If they truly had commitment to Him, they must walk the walk and go see the priest.

It's no different with us today. Jesus is watching to see if we're ready to "walk the walk." Immediately, when we put our faith in Christ, we are cleansed, but He wants to see us put feet to our faith. James puts it this way: "Yea, a man say, Thou hast faith, and I have works: shew me your faith without thy works, and I will shew thee my faith by my works" (James 2:18). God wants our faith, but He wants us to put it to work. These lepers had to transfer from the talk of faith to the step of faith. Without further discussion, they were to get into gear and show their healing to the priests—before the actual healing had even taken place. Again, we are to do the same in life. We need to show Jesus Christ that we are putting our faith into action, thus letting Him work His plan that He has for us through us. He doesn't tell us where we are going to be in life or how He is going to work it all out. We are simply placed in the position of believing that He has it all under control. Will He heal us at the beginning of our walk in faith, at the middle, or late in our travels through life? We need only realize that He has already provided us with the cure and healing. We need only step forward in faith. For these lepers, their faith was tested in that they were being told to trust the directives given by God in Leviticus 14. If they trusted and went to the priests, they would be healed.

In the case of the ten lepers, their healing must have been nigh on immediate. There was no doubt that it came to pass. As they were putting their feet to work and their faith to the test, they were cleansed of leprosy. Their faith had not been misplaced. Jesus had healed them. The anticipation of healing that these lepers had up to the point of healing must have been electric. Their senses must have been piqued. All of them, looking at their own skin as they travelled, had to have been hugely expectant.

Somewhere between here and there, they knew that the healing had to happen. Like us, they just didn't know when it would take place. Yes, for some of us, healing will not occur physically here on earth, but rather in heaven. We know that and see it everywhere. The attitude, though, that He wants us to have is one of already walking in the healing. No, it's not "name it and claim it" but is our walking through life knowing that He has already changed our lives and attitudes. He has given us the knowledge that we will one day be physically whole (Revelation 22:2) but are spiritually whole right now. We must be thankful for this promise of healing, knowing that His healing of our mind and spirit is of far more consequence than any physical healing could ever be.

## LUKE 17:11-19
*Verse 15*

It seems that only one of the ten lepers understood this concept of spiritual healing. He saw that he was healed. Turning around, he came back to Christ and loudly and gratefully gave God the glory for the healing. Yes, he was most assuredly still planning to go and show himself to the priests, as directed, but he had to give thanks to the Person of Jesus Christ; the One who had provided his healing.

This man knew who had supplied the cure. It came from God. Straightforwardly, this ex-leper knew that God deserved the credit for the cure. As we've seen already, only God could heal leprosy. He knew that his first duty would be to give thanks to the Lord God who was able to cleanse an unclean leper. After giving thanks, one can then give due to the law, as was the situation in the time of Christ and these ten lepers.

Giving credit to God is not a private thing. This is contrary to the view of many today who state that one's faith is a matter of personal conscience and is, therefore, not to be shared with those around them. This leper, a Samaritan, as we will find out, had the correct approach to thanksgiving. He proclaimed it loudly. The whole crowd had viewed Christ's handling of the lepers, and now the whole crowd saw and heard this man's thankfulness and glorification of God. It was his personal testimony that would be proclaimed for the remainder of his life, and for that matter in heaven, of the fact that God had healed and cleansed him. Are we as thankful today of the blessings supplied to us: healing, food, clothing, shelter, jobs, and the like? How many today even give thanks to the Lord for food placed in front of them at each meal?

## LUKE 17:11-19
*Verse 16*

This man's act of thankfulness was fit for a king. He fell down on his face at Jesus' feet. This was an act of adoration. He was worshipping Jesus Christ, the Son of God. It may be this world's methodology to touch a knee to the floor and bow one's head while addressing or thanking a king of a realm of this world. In this case, though, this Samaritan was acknowledging Christ's Lordship over him. This Samaritan had finished the equation. Only God can heal lepers. Christ Jesus healed the lepers. Therefore, Christ is God. Notice, too, that Jesus Christ accepted the adoration and worship without correcting the Samaritan ex-leper. He didn't stop the leper by saying, "Don't worship me! Only God above is to be worshipped." He accepted the act of worship and then began a rhetorical conversation with this man and, really, with the crowd listening around them.

Before we leave this verse, a definition of "Samaritan" is in order. A Samaritan was a person born in the region just north of Jerusalem— Samaria, the area first given to Ephraim when the Israelites occupied the land of Canaan after their Egyptian captivity and forty years in the wilderness[22]. About 700 years before Christ, the Jews were at war with Assyria. When Assyria won and Jews were taken into captivity in Assyria, many Assyrians came down to take possession of this Samarian region. Over the years, hostilities ended, and the Jews were able to come back to their old region. Over time, Jews intermarried with Assyrians, creating a new half-Jew race called Samaritans. Other full-blooded Jews surrounding the Samarian area would, in future centuries, look down on them as mixed-blood Gentiles[23]. Jews would even look down on them as people who participated in the Jewish religion but worshipped in the wrong location of Mount Gerizim in Samaria and not at the proper location of the temple in Jerusalem (John 4:20-22)[24].

So, here was this mixed-blood, Gentile Samaritan who had been cleansed of leprosy and was now at Christ's feet submitting to Him in worship and thanks. Is it because he was simply thankful and wanted to give God the direct credit? Is it because this Samaritan was not used to worshipping in Jerusalem and did not have legal and emotional ties to the temple of the Jews? Is it because the nine other ex-lepers discouraged his participation and certification of his now "non-leprous condition" at the temple because there was no longer a tie of leprosy among the ten? We're not told. Jesus would make a comment in the verses to come that may shed light on this situation.

## LUKE 17:11-19

*Verse 17*

Jesus began a conversation that would turn out to be one-sided. He received no comment from the Samaritan ex-leper. Wisely, the Samaritan did not comment regarding the lack of thankfulness of his former compatriots in the "sin" of leprosy. Jesus received no comment from the crowd gathered around them. He received no comment from

His disciples, and specifically no comment or answer was offered by His apostles. This is one of those rare instances when the Apostle Peter had nothing to say.

Jesus, evidently saddened by the lack of gratitude, sees only ten percent of the leprous group return to offer praise and thanks. It makes one ask if there is significance to this number. Is only ten percent of the world's population thankful to the work Jesus Christ has done for them? The analogy becomes stretched here if we go too far, but is this a representative number indicating the final number of people who will be saved to eternal life with Jesus Christ? Or, is it significant that a Gentile offers Christ thanks for His wonderful work, a member of an "other-than-Jew-race" that would be used of God when Israel fully rejected Jesus as the Messiah? This is a rejection that has lasted almost two thousand years, but the Word assures us that this rejection will not last much longer (Ezekiel 39:7, 13, 22, 29).

It is a serious thing to ponder. Nine of the ten do not return to give Christ thanks for giving them their lives back by cleansing them. How quickly mankind forgets the mercies supplied to them by the Lord. Disasters strike, but man does not thank the Lord when He brings them through the flood, the hurricane, the earthquake, the fire, and such. Always, it is our duty to thank God for trials. Romans 5:3 makes it clear that trials in life assist us in learning patience (1 Peter 5:10). They're not fun, though it is clear that we are going to go through them (John 16:33, 2 Timothy 3:10-12).

Jesus is said to have viewed the tribulation of the cross as joy because He was soon to pass through the shame of His suffering and then be able to sit down at the right hand of His Father again (Hebrews 12:2). That must have been a joyful reunion! One of the things that Paul clarifies is that we need to give thanks in everything, and that includes both the good and the bad, since our going through these things is God's will for us (1 Thessalonians 5:18). We must have the faith that God is in control and that He will preserve us, spirit, soul, and body (1 Thessalonians 5:23, 24). He will accomplish the work in us, regardless of the dire circumstances in which we presently find ourselves.

## LUKE 17:11-19

*Verse 18*

Christ makes it clear that He is displeased that only one who received a miraculous healing has come back to give glory to God. Leprosy is a horrible disease, but only one of the men who were saved from leprosy's destructive grasp made the choice to return to humbly thank the Master Healer. The ingratitude here is that the men who did not return were, in blood, His countrymen. They had called Him "Master" but seem not to have believed that they owed Him thanks for restoring their health and cleansing them from the dreaded disease. He needed to be thanked for their salvation from the nasty death that leprosy, or its resultant and related problems, would have dealt them. Again, they were likely not very far down the road and could readily have come back to thank Him. Only one did return to offer the thanks that the Lord Jesus deserved.

Christ calls him "this stranger," meaning that he is a foreigner and not a Jew. In many ways, this man was an alien in an alien land. Even Christ Jesus refers to him as a stranger. Christ and His followers were passing through Samaria and Galilee and, even though he was theoretically the "local guy," the Samaritan was considered the stranger. It's as if Jesus did not expect him to know the etiquette of gratitude, though the Jews should have. Yet the stranger was the thankful one. The Samaritan was so thankful that Christ was probably still looking down at the back of the Samaritan's head!

This man knew what he had been saved from and realized that this healing was his "ticket" out of a horrible death. Not only that, but the stigma of deep sin would now be expunged, cleared from his record. He would no longer be cold, hungry, homeless, and poor, and would again be accepted by his family. Maybe he had a wife and children awaiting him. Maybe the list of people to whom he could return included his parents. Maybe he could go home to a job from which he had been terminated. People might make reference to him in the future as "The Leper," but only because he had been a leper. When Jesus sets us free, we are truly free and do not have to live the old life (John 8:36). This man had lived a horrible life and knew now that he was freed from it. He could now go home.

## LUKE 17:11-19
*Verse 19*

This matter of the cure of ten lepers ends with an interesting development. Jesus speaks to the leper, who must still be on his face, and tells him to arise and go his way. The Samaritan is informed that his faith has now made him whole. Didn't the other nine have faith? They had immediately turned and started their trek to the priests to receive their certification of cleansing. They had called Jesus "Master," signifying their belief and trust in Him and the fact that He was the Lord of their lives, reigning and ruling over them for eternity.

Jesus' statement raises the question about their "wholeness." Were they saved when they had their healing from Christ? We honestly have no way to know that. It may be, instead, that we have a situation. Is this a situation where the other nine were crying the equivalent of "Lord, Lord!" and acting hypocritical, as in Luke 6:46? Here is the story of Jesus giving a talk on "The Plain." In verse 45, he mentions the heart of men who truly do good things, and the speech of this kind of man belies the real heart underneath. In other words, if a man speaks well and truly does good things, it may be assumed that the man is good inside and out—clearly a man of God. But, the man who does not do good things, yet speaks good things, is not really a good man. He is not a man of God. The man who is not good is building a house on sand, doomed for destruction (Luke 6:49), while the man who is good in God is building on rock, able to withstand the storms of life (Luke 6:48). Many people do well and fake us out. Are the nine like these?

Or, is this another "Lord, Lord" situation from Matthew 7:23? Here, Jesus Christ talks about the final judgment where all will one day acknowledge Him in heaven. They say, "Lord, Lord!" to Him, but He rejects them. He acknowledges that they've done all sorts of good things in His name, though He still does not know them. They had never truly given Him their allegiance and asked Him to take over their lives. Again, Matthew equates these men to builders of houses, some on sand, and some on solid rock (Matthew 7:24-27).

Let's take this analysis one step further. The nine lepers cried, "Jesus, Master!" Were they truly men who had truly repented of sinful pasts and committed their lives to Christ, or were they simply men who wanted to try to fake Jesus—and God—out and thus receive healing? This last verse dealing with the ten lepers, verse 19, now seems to indicate that they only received physical healing. The nine did not have gratitude in their hearts. The Lord reads our hearts, and these nine evidently did not pass muster in Jesus' view (1 Samuel 16:7). It would seem that the Samaritan leper not only received physical healing, but spiritual healing too. He was made whole in both his body and soul. His actions showed his true heart for Christ, while the hearts of the other nine betrayed by their lack of thankfulness to Jesus Christ. Essentially, the nine cried, "Lord, Lord!" but their hearts were not with Him.

Maybe the situation is that these nine lepers are like so many people around us who want what Jesus Christ has to offer without really wanting to be personally straightened out. They want healing without repentance, liking their own sinful ways of life more than loving

God. They want to give verbal obeisance and not a change of heart, no turning from their sinful pasts.

Too many want the better life with God. They do not, however, want to commit to a life where their sinful past is eradicated and the hard work of walking with Christ begins. This becomes serious. There are truly only two outcomes to the choice one makes about sin. We spend eternity somewhere. Heaven and hell are the only two alternatives.

Let's discuss the effects of leprosy, comparing leprosy to these sins and the associated life of sin.

# 4: AN INFECTIOUS DISEASE

When we take a serious look at leprosy, it becomes clear that there have been real problems with the treatment of those who suffered with the disease through the centuries, at least up until the 1900s. We understand why this has been so. So little was known about what it was or how it was acquired. And then, when a person was found to be infected, it was already too late. The person was forced into isolation and was "branded" unclean. So why was the disease considered a punishment for the individual's sin? We can draw some comparisons between leprosy and sin.

True leprosy, as previously discussed, can lie dormant in one's system for as long as thirty years. It is dormant and hidden from its host for so long that the infected person has no idea where it came from or at what point he or she was infected. At some point, it just showed up, and now the individual is sick. Is sin any different?

The Word is repetitive, singing the same tune throughout Scripture, when it comes to the origin of sin in a person's life. We are born with it (Psalm 51:5). Sin is in our hearts and thus engenders all types of problems like evil thoughts, murders, adulteries (sexual intercourse between a spouse and one who is not the marriage partner), fornications (sexual intercourse between those who are not married), thefts, false witnesses (telling lies about others), and blasphemies (calling God down to our level by using His name irreverently) as seen in Matthew 15:19. The Word even points out that wars really come from lusts within a man's heart, the desire to have what is someone else's (James 4:1).

We are born with the desire to do what we want to do in life, fulfilling our own wants instead of determining what God has directed for our lives. In other words, we don't want to listen to His commands and would rather not live by His standards. We are well on our way to setting our own standards in life even before we ever realize that our hearts are rebellious.

So, one day we awake to the fact that we are sinful—and don't in fact understand that we were infected with sin from day one, just like the leper who awakens to find that the disease has taken control of his or her life. For a while, a leper can hide the illness. There may be spots on the skin that have turned numb. They're insensitive and unaffected by another's touch or the extremes of heat or cold. The prick of a pin draws no sense of pain. The skin is essentially saying, "I don't care anymore." The leper continues on in life with decreased feeling, thus withdrawing from the pains and extremes of life.

The numbness brought about by sin is similar to that brought about by leprosy. The evil of sin no longer affects the senses of the sinner. The conscience is dulled, and "little sins" are shrugged off as being no problem. The white lie is viewed as something needful to save someone's feelings or to escape an embarrassing moment where one does not want to be accountable for his or her actions, when the truth is that it is a lie and therefore a sin. As the illness of sin grows, so do the dullness and lack of sensitivity. If unchecked, the sin grows deeper within the infected "leper." But, for now, the effects of sin are still hidden.

Numbness is growing within the leper, but, since it's not visible, it remains known only to the leper. Rashes and flaky skin now begin to appear. Most likely, a patch of this rash is on one's back, or on the thigh, or maybe on the forearm. One may be able to cover it with clothing—a long sleeve shirt or long pants. To the infected, this stage is embarrassing and not likely diagnosed as leprosy. The sufferer simply knows that there is a rash and some spots with odd numbness and tingling. The disease is relatively easy to hide.

Since it is undiagnosed, self-medication is now underway. Ointments for the rash bring temporary relief of the flaking skin. Self-massage of the areas that are numb, again, may bring temporary tingling and relief. No relief is permanent with leprosy, though. The disease progresses and spreads. Without proper diagnosis and treatment, leprosy will take the infected person to levels of the illness that are unable to be hidden and are irreversible. The leprosy will soon be apparent.

And again, sin is similar in its ability to be hidden by the sinner, the infected one. Small lies create larger lies. Small unfaithfulness creates greater unfaithfulness. Little thefts grow into larger thefts. Sexual lusts grow from those things done in the dark at home to those done in public and involving other people. For a time, those things may remain unseen and lied about. One has the sin "under control" and is able to stop for a time in order to keep from being found out. For example, one can work at a job and not allow alcohol use to affect his work activity. After work, though, the "medicinal use" of the alcohol must start in order to soothe those nerves that are jangled from a hard day's work. Those nerves must be numbed. The alcoholic can imbibe under the guise of enjoying time out with friends at the bar, covering the growing addiction and sin. They're simply out having a good time, right? But, the need for alcohol is growing and is now being used quietly and secretly at home, concealed by the four walls. Eventually, though, that hidden alcoholism will be revealed.

It's quite easy to substitute the sin involved by simply replacing any sin stated above with one's sin of choice. Is it drugs? The drug user, seemingly more often than not, starts the downward slide by enjoying the drug at parties and with groups of friends who state that they are simply having a good time. The drug simply helps them relax and get loose, they say. Whatever the drug involved, be it cocaine, crack, pain killers, heroin, or any other drug, it will take over with higher frequency and amounts needed for the drug user to get the original "high" experienced when he first took the drug. When the addict loses control, there is no more hiding the effect that the specific problem is having on the person's life.

Once the disease became visible, the physically-infected leper was forced to isolate himself from the center of society. Because he became known to be infectious and sick, he was eliminated from family gatherings and was no longer able to participate as an active family member. The family wanted nothing to do with the leper. What if the infection was relayed to the children? How could someone so hideous be allowed to sit around the house and act as if nothing was wrong? The family and surrounding community had to get rid of him.

Lepers were forced into wearing clothing that flagged them as lepers, covering their lower faces, and shouting, "Unclean! Unclean!" when they were around others. Clearly, some secret sin had forced them to receive this punishment from God, and they must go off and pay for their sins. Isn't this what happens to those who are completely taken with their sins today?

A husband, a wife, children, and parents see the signs that their family member is completely taken with their addiction or sin—spiritual leprosy. The boss and coworkers see the degrading work quality, the poor attendance, and the dilated eyes or smell the alcohol on the breath. All see a person who is losing his grasp on what has mattered to him in the past, who no longer seems to care. If kept nearby, he will affect the work of others or destroy the relationship of the family.

Sooner or later, the ultimatum is given to either straighten up his life or get out.

With their sins now so visible, most simply get out. Most of the time, they don't even agree with their family or bosses. They do not view themselves as being out of control or addicted. They feel they have a handle on their lives and do not need help from anyone, so they leave, isolated and—in their minds—misunderstood.

What do the lepers do when unceremoniously removed from the life they have known? They go to locations where other lepers have gathered, joining into a band of sick misfits. Here's the problem. We've already covered the fact that many "lepers" may not be lepers after all. Those who are will stay in the group until something drastic occurs. It might be their death due to complications that have arisen from their own leprosy. It may be that they are one day healed by God. When they join the group, they do not know their future.

So, suppose some are not actually leprous. They may have one of those illnesses that we had previously mentioned, like lupus, psoriasis, syphilis, or ringworm. Being misdiagnosed as having leprosy, they are now in a real bind. They are relegated to staying with their leprous friends. They are exposed to all of the maladies represented within the group. Who knows? If they didn't have leprosy when they arrived, they may well become infected, just like Fr. Damien. Maybe they will contract syphilis from within the group, making their personal situation even worse.

Say they are leprous. As their disease progresses, they are prone to having open sores that do not heal. Their bodies are not working well anymore. Their runny noses, their sores, the ulcers on their feet all become possible points of intake to those diseases being shared within the group. The obvious result is that all of the "lepers" are now becoming worse off simply by their association within the group. The leper is also sharing his leprosy with others, as stated above. Their "scourge" is becoming permanent, regardless of the ailment that they had when they arrived.

The comparison to spiritual leprosy is readily seen. Though often the sinner leaves his home to get away from family members who increasingly get on his case because he is not correcting his life's problems, or the boss has told the employee to leave due to work problems, he now becomes involved with others who may not share the same addictions. Though he may have arrived with a drug problem, he may acquire problems with alcohol, sex, theft, and many other maladies to which he is exposed. For example, theft may be "acquired" because he must now support a habit. It's possible that he was stealing from family and friends before he left their homes, a situation that those families were not very happy about. The downward spiral that he was already experiencing is now spiraling even harder out of control. His life is filled with corruption and lies, just like the leper whose body is coming apart. He is experiencing pain, disfigurement, degraded bodily functions, and social ostracism as a result of his sin.

For the leper, death is not far away. No longer receiving good, nutritious food, he is weakening physically. Blindness is setting in as the leprosy advances. Internal organs are shutting down due to the disease's progress. Infections are now numerous aside from the leprosy because of exposed tissues at locations of his ulcers, especially on his feet. He is becoming less mobile, his limbs less useful as the disfigurement becomes extreme. Hands are turning into inflexible claws. Feet are ulcerated and disfigured, no longer able to support the weight of his emaciated body. In an effort to stay mobile, he walks with a stick to prop himself up, or he crawls across the ground. Other infections he has acquired from people around him are now taking a severe toll on his body. Things like psoriasis, syphilis, lung diseases, and the like are dragging him down rapidly.

Once dead, the bodies of commoners who could not afford tombs or burial plots were normally gathered and buried in a mass grave outside the city. In Jerusalem, this was a place called Gehenna, a place on the city's outskirts named "the Valley of the Son of Hinnom." In the Old Testament times, this was a place where those who followed the religion of the god Molech would burn their children alive in the sacrificial fires of the valley of the son of Hinnom—Gehenna (2 Kings 23:10). Thus, it would become a place that people viewed as a type of hell, torment, and judgment, burning and consuming the bodies both of those who were alive and those who were dead (Jeremiah 7:32, 19:6). Later, it is reputed to have become a dump for the city's rubbish, with fires constantly burning,[25] likely burning the city's dead who died as paupers or ne'er-do-wells. Luke even quotes Jesus as He refers to Gehenna in his Gospel in Luke 12:5 saying,

> *But I will forewarn you whom ye shall fear: Fear Him, which after He hath killed hath power to cast into hell; yea, I say unto you, Fear Him.*

Figuratively speaking, the leper had only to look forward to his own death and picture himself being burned in the fires of Gehenna. Here, his body was falling apart, he was sick, and he had only flames of fire to which to look forward. His "punishment" continued, in his mind, even after death.

The picture of the "sinner as leper" is again clear. The sinner who abandons himself to a life of self-service and sin deteriorates throughout the end of his life. His life falls apart. No one wants to help him, hoping that the shock of being totally abandoned will bring the sinner to his knees and ultimately to repentance. But, if the sinner does not repent, the addictions he or she has now come to hate have—in effect—buried the individual alive. Life has become about getting that next "fix," whether it is a drug, sex, or a drink. Nothing else matters any more, not even health.

The Bible calls such individuals the servants of sin, and this is a bondage that leads to death (Romans 6:17). They stand at a cross-road. Either they decide to follow their path of sin to destruction that lasts for eternity, Gehenna, or they choose to come out from being a servant to sin and follow the path of repentance that leads to their salvation at Calvary. In other words, they must become servants of God in order to spend eternity in heaven. At its most basic element, this is a choice. It's a choice to rely on their own selves for eternity, or to rely on Jesus Christ and His work for eternity.

At some point in time, these people believed themselves free, at liberty to do as they pleased. The alcohol, the drugs, the sex, and all of their other lusts created a sense of freedom that allowed them to believe that they could do anything with their lives that they desired, and no one or nothing could make them accountable to a soul, not even to God. Peter puts it this way in his second epistle:

For when they speak great swelling words of vanity, they allure through the lusts of the flesh, through much wantonness, those that were clean escaped from them who live in error. While they promise them liberty, they themselves are the servants of corruption: for of whom a man is overcome, of the same is he brought in bondage (2 Peter 2:18-19).

Verse 18 clarifies for us that some will escape and get out of the corruption and away from those who are living in wanton error. It can be done. People can and do get out of the death spiral that is akin to leprosy. But, in verse 19, others view their sin as liberty: license to sin all the more. Instead, they have become servants to their addictions; their corruptions. And then, they are overcome by bondage or slavery to the sin they once loved. Without a willing turnaround, they will die in their sins and will eternally reside in a place called Gehenna.

# 5: A DISEASE RUN RAMPANT

n the chapter three, we talked about the jobs those ten lepers may have held when they were in their "previous lives." They might have been craftsmen, professionals like doctors and lawyers, business managers, or engineers, at least in today's terms regarding jobs. Now, from a spiritual aspect, let's look at the types of sin in their lives.

What kind of sinners are spiritual lepers today? Regardless of who we are and whether we're living as Christians or unbelievers, there is a battle raging within every human being. We have a lust within us called the "lust of the flesh." As Christians, we have the assistance of the Holy Spirit residing in us to aid us in our resistance to the lust of the flesh. Paul spells this out in Galatians 5:17. The verse directly before that, Galatians 5:16, states that walking in the Spirit does not allow one to walk in these lusts. The Holy Spirit is the key. Unbelievers do not have the Holy Spirit's assistance. It's all left up to the unbelievers themselves. As it turns out, their own power can't do the job of keeping them straight (out of sin). Instead, their lives show the indelible signs of sin that runs rampant within them. They cannot control their lives and don't really even know what is right and what is classified as wrong. Proverbs 14:12 puts it this way: "There is a way that seemeth right unto a man, but the end thereof are the ways of death." Even the things that they believe to be good and right in life don't please God. They just have no idea what it takes to please God. Their own ways will lead to an eternal death in hell.

In previous portions of this book, we've talked only minimally of specific sins. Paul provides details in the book of Galatians. We want to know what these "spiritual lepers" are into—what keeps them in bondage. Why is it that they cannot get closer to God, and why can't they know what is controlling their lives? When one itemizes and studies this list, the reader realizes that no one can control the actions they take unless they do have the Holy Spirit giving them aid and counsel, both through the Bible that gives them the details to understand what godliness is and through the Holy Spirit who is the "still small voice" in their ears (1 Kings 19:12).

A list of our "bad deeds" is sizeable. And, in many ways, we can all admit to a bit of guilt in each one of them. We can now go to a study that looks at these "deeds" of sin. Knowing that we're all sinners, let's take a look at Paul's list from Galatians 5:19-21.

> *Now the works of the flesh are manifest, which are these: Adultery, fornication, uncleanness, lasciviousness, idolatry, witchcraft, hatred, variance, emulations, wrath, strife, seditions, heresies, envyings, murders, drunkenness, revellings, and such like: of the which I tell you before, as I have also told you in time past, that they which do such things shall not inherit the kingdom of God.*

Watching those around us, we see traits that start to emerge from within these people. These traits indicate the status of the hearts of these people. No, this is not judgment of them or their souls. We simply use our sense of discernment to see whether or not they have a relationship with God. We neither have the duty nor the ability to determine what is in a person's heart, as we see in 1 Corinthians

5:9-13. In this 1 Corinthians passage, Paul makes it clear that we are not to spend large amounts of time with people who are living in sins like fornication, covetousness, idolatry, and so on, since we do not want their "leprous sins" to rub off on us. To many, this may seem to be judgmental, but it is not. In verses 12 and 13, the word judge is aimed at judicial judgment.[26] We do not have the right to judge people's souls regarding whether they will be eternally in heaven or hell. We have only the duty of discerning or evaluating their actions to know whether we should or should not spend time with them (1 Corinthians 2:15).[27] We do not know if those around us are saved, but we can watch for these indicators to show us how we can help them by sharing the Good News, the gospel, with them. We need to do our part to win the lost to Christ.

Let's move to an analysis of the Galatians 5:19-21 passage. We can look at these sins and have a relatively accurate and detailed picture of the spiritual leper. These lepers are doing all sorts of things that cause them to stand further away from the crowd of society—in essence, joining in with their fellow lepers. When studying the individual sins portrayed here, be aware that these actions are not referring to the occasional mistake. They are describing the actions of a person who is sold out to these categorized sins. We'll apply the word "abandoned" to the sin in order to show the extent to which these people are becoming more covered and deformed with their chosen leprous conditions. Additionally, their conditions are starting to spread and overlap into other sins as they pick up the maladies of their fellow lepers. The infection is running rampant as it tears their own and others' lives apart.

## ADULTERY

*(moicheia: adultery)*

Again, this word points to a number of acts of adultery, meaning that it is a lifestyle[28]. It's not just the occasional incident of sexual intercourse between a spouse and a person who is not the other spouse. These people are given over to this act of sin. It's destroying not only them but also their marriages and families. In this age of "open marriage," God's standards for the family are being torn down. The scourge on this leper is severe due to the damage done as one goes against God's unchanging standards.

## FORNICATION

*(porneia: harlotry, adultery, incest, fornication, to the level of idolatry)*

This word covers a multitude of sins that are unsanctioned by God's Word. Acts such as sexual intercourse outside of marriage, prostitution, being "unchaste" or having given up one's virtue, and fornication which is sexual intercourse outside of marriage.[29] The Greek root word "porno" is where the English language picks up the word "pornography." With magazines, movies, the Internet, X-rated bookstores, and all manner of advertisements selling sex, it tells us that today's worldwide, sexually-driven culture is dragging down both men and women into the moral abyss. Called "free speech," the world's morals, and specifically America's morals, are now degraded to the point that most people are hardened to it. It is no longer fornication or pornography, but is deemed as legal, whether it be for women, men, and, lately, even children in many parts of the world. This is a scourge and the world has spiritual leprosy for it.

## UNCLEANNESS

*(akatharsia: physical and moral impurity)*

This is a state of moral corruption that implies immorality and vileness in sexual sins. These people are delving into all kinds of sexual sins that have made them totally unclean. Their morals have completely collapsed.[30] They are completely given over to sex and all of its related lusts. These lepers are truly unclean.

## LASCIVIOUSNESS
*(aselgeia: a person who is completely wanton in their filthy vices)*

Here, we are talking about sexual excesses that are up to the level of total abandonment with the person having no self-constraint. This word indicates that the person has passed beyond all levels of social acceptability and is totally given himself over to self-abandonment to sex.[31]

## IDOLATRY
*(eidololatreia: image worship)*

Society has many gods today, and many individuals worship several of these lesser gods.[32] Actually, it's easy to list common idols that mankind worships: money and wealth, power, sex, material goods like cars and homes, beauty, drugs, alcohol, entertainment, leisure, knowledge, and the list goes on. People are worshipping "self." In essence, mankind has set himself up as a god to be served. Rather than spending a life in service to God and his fellow man, he is serving himself in order to get the most from life for himself. It is all greed and self-service when, in God's view, man is to be serving and worshipping Him (Psalm 95:6, Matthew 4:10).

## WITCHCRAFT
*(pharmakeia: medication, pharmacy, magic, witchcraft, sorcery)*

One may not immediately tie the terms of witchcraft to pharmaceuticals or drugs. When one realizes that they complement each other quite well, the link begins to appear. Today's culture has taken the old idea of witchcraft and sorcery to an all new level. The Greek word used here is taken by the English language as the word pharmacy, or pharmaceuticals and drugs.[33] But, it's translated as witchcraft and sorcery in the Bible, and it's easy to understand why.

Drugs readily numb the mind, causing the person to think less clearly. Essentially, today's anti-depressants, uppers, downers, and so on create a "mood" for a person that allows him or her to "chill out" and avoid addressing problems in life, wholly given to just "feeling good." Extended to drugs like heroin, cocaine, methamphetamines, and the like, the individual is taken to new highs of ecstasy that are only temporary, and thus new fixes and increasing doses are mandated by the user to get that original sense of euphoria. The old small dose just doesn't give the "kick" needed to move into that much-needed "la-la land."

When one is on prescribed drugs for the handling of depression, emotions (like sadness, anger, anxieties, and physical pain) no longer need to be addressed. The individual is medicated to the level that these emotions simply go away. The problem is that they are not truly gone, just temporarily submerged. Maturity for the individual has not developed—the individual has not had to learn to work through problems in life. Maturity is delayed until the individual is slowly taken off of the drug.

However, society and the medical community have found that it's easier to prescribe a pill than to deal with an issue. It's easy to concoct the potion and cast the spell on "the sufferer." Today, the patient needs only say, "I'm depressed," in order to qualify for the desired drugs. Prison populations, school populations, and social welfare populations are given these drugs not as much for the population itself, but to avoid spending time and money working with individuals to determine what the real problem is. In short, the real problem may be a heart full of sin and godlessness (Jeremiah 17:9). Knowing the Lord in a saving way opens the exit door to grow out of these "mind problems." In other words, the only way to exit the drug problem that society has today is to turn our focus away from self and up to God. In our study, these medicines have masked the leprosy, but have not cured it.

Lest we go too far on this subject, let's be reminded that there are some legitimate uses or needs for those drugs that address problems within one's brain. Brain damage due to accidents, birth defects, and the like, do merit the use of medicines that control all sorts of things: seizures, verbal outbursts, uncontrollable emotions, and so on. But, the reasoning here is measured and the need is indicated with proper medical analysis and tests. On the other hand, prescriptions for anti-depressants and the like are often given on the basis of interviews with the patient without conducting medical tests such as blood analysis.[34] My point is that medicine may possibly be needed for a short period of time whether for pain, trauma, deep emotional concerns, and so forth, but the patient needs to be weaned from the drug as he or she is given a full diet of the Word that demonstrates how to live.

Here is the main point. The "spells" cast by man on his fellow man will not cure one's bondage to sin as a spiritual leper. It will only lull the user into complacency, making the user think that all is well in life. The pills and drugs prescribed are only placebos to make the person believe that wellness is being restored. This is not how one is made well spiritually. Instead, the only eternal option is to be cured by the Lord, just as He provides the only real cure for leprosy.

## HATRED

*(echthra: hostility, a reason for opposition, enmity)*

Hatred or enmity is hostile feelings and actions toward people.[35] Some people are openly hostile to those who simply oppose them. In many ways, the reasons do not matter. In fact, by the time "hate" is in place, all of the real reasons for ill will between two or more people have gone by the wayside. Blindness has set in. The person who hates is transformed into ugliness, deformed by loathing for the individual experiences of someone else. The spiritual leprosy grows more serious and deforming.

## VARIANCE

*(eris: a quarrel, wrangling, contention, debate, strife)*

When a rivalry occurs between people, this is the person who likes to take sides in order to create more contention.[36] The person is quarrelsome and enjoys causing strife. He or she is at "variance" with people, maybe not even knowing the reason why. This contentious person is at odds with society and is forced as a consequence of personal choices into a leprous group that will stand afar off and scream at the mainstream of society.

## EMULATIONS

*(zelos: jealousy, as in jealousy of God or an enemy; envy, zealously jealous)*

This person hates other people's achievements and is extremely jealous, envying the success of others.[37] Emulations is easily tied to variance above, in that an ungodly rivalry is created and an enemy is created, even if it's only one way and the other person does not reinforce or support the competition. As the emulators stand in their "far off group," they are jealous of everyone but do not know how to get back into society to receive the cure. They believe that everyone but them knows how to get along and are jealous of what they perceive to be others' prosperity. And, they're enthusiastic about their jealousy, too. This person blames God for the other person's wealth and success, and does so loudly. The lepers are calling from the crowd, demanding equality, though they have not worked for it and don't deserve it.

## WRATH

*(thumos: passionately fierce, indignation)*

Wrath is expressed by this person by showing intense displeasure and anger, with outbursts of rage and indignation.[38] Again, this shows the constant anger and rage expressed by the person and reveals that it is a lifestyle. They are the lepers who are blaming God for their own plight, when their plight might have been sent their way to help straighten them out and wake them up. They are lepers who are angry at the world, though they have created their own leprosy.

## STRIFE
*(eritheia: intrigue implying faction, contention)*

One might simply call this problem selfishness.[39] Strife occurs when the person reveals selfish ambition through disputes. The person is contentious with those who are perceived by him or her as getting to the top first. This individual will fight and contend for the position that belongs to someone else. In this contest for advancement, strivers are only hurting themselves and causing their leprosy to grow as their own infections get worse.

## SEDITIONS
*(dichostasia: disunion, division, dissension)*

Here, the individual is causing dissent and opposition.[40] This is the type of person who is chipping away at causes or maybe even a person's reputation; the person being discredited may not even know that it is being done against them. By causing this "disunion," seditionists are creating the degradation of their own bodies as they advance the leprous sores within themselves.

## HERESIES
*(hairesis: a choice, party, or disunion)*

This is a group that holds views that are distinctive and counter to the main group. This is a party or sect that knowingly does not adhere to the doctrines of Christianity, and they are doing so negatively in dissent from these doctrines.[41] Even in Paul's day, people were subtracting and adding to the gospel in order to suit their personal needs—in knowing opposition to Jesus Christ. Today, it is occurring on a mass scale. One must be wary of the doctrine being preached by many churches today. Many are no longer doctrinally correct. In order for the "doctrinal society" to survive, this group of leprous heretics must be sent away from society in order for society not to be infected. Churches must keep the lepers from infecting the whole doctrinal society.

## ENVYINGS
*(phthonos: ill will, jealousy, spite, envy)*

This is pure jealousy and envy of another.[42] Maybe it's because someone is prettier, popular, or smarter, or maybe for no cognizant reason at all. In Titus 3:3, the word is used among other character traits where the person is serving her own diverse lusts and is simply living in a state of malice, envy, and hate of other people. Sometimes, one doesn't really need a reason to dislike and be envious of others. It's done out of a feeling of spite. This is the leper who may know about the cure, but stands back and envies others' health just to spite them.

## MURDERS
*(phonos: murder, to be slain, slaughter)*

This is what it is: the slaying of another human being. A person is murdered in an action using the deadly edge of a sword or other weapon.[43] There does not have to be a reason for doing so. Even if the recipient of the blow still lives, the murderer may have acted by wrongly destroying the person's reputation and the like. In a murderous spirit, the killer has murdered his own leprous self.

## DRUNKENNESS
*(methe: intoxicant, intoxication)*

This view of drunkenness not only seems to include the idea of being drunk but also involves the constant and personally destructive use of alcohol.[44] Placed in the list near "revellings," it includes the party or "drinking bout" situation, drinking with revelry. This person takes the use of alcohol to the limits of "self-medication," just like the person who is using drugs to wipe out all feeling. The leprosy is covered over, and the pain is temporarily removed, but the disease continues to grow.

## REVELLINGS
*(komos: carousal, letting loose, rioting)*

This word is associated with the partying and carousing that goes with excessive feasting and revelry.[45] These people have let their emotions run wild and are living a lifestyle that has gone past having fun, food, and fellowship. This group has moved past the point of good judgment to the level of rioting, where counting the cost of damage, both to self and surroundings, is no longer considered. At any time where drugs, alcohol, and emotions are unleashed, one quickly arrives at the gate of self-destruction. Whether through accidental personal harm, contracted disease (as in the case of drug use and sexual contact), or property damage, this revelling has taken the place of good judgment and is now running that person's life. The reveler is out of control. The spiritual leprosy has completely broken the body down and has created a walking and talking individual devoid of all feeling.

## AND SUCH LIKE?
*(toigaroun: consequently, therefore; homoiosis: similar in character)*

Galatians 5:21 places these two words together to make the point that more of these traits can be implied,[46] and we can pick up like resemblances[47] to other sin in life. Obviously, we can combine the traits listed above with each other. Paul is giving us a bit of license here to recognize that other traits do exist that could be added to the list. Greed or covetousness is inherent to many of these traits, though it is not specifically listed above. Selfishness has been used and could individually be listed. The characteristics of sin could fill volumes. We could even go to other lists of sin within the Bible, but this is a reasonably comprehensive list for our purposes.

The last portion of verse 21 indicates the severity of such sins when carried to extremes as we've seen above. These are people who habitually do such things, behaving with abandon. When they act with abandon and without correcting their errant lifestyles, they are assured that they will not inherit the kingdom of God, which is heaven. Let's now go into this thought on sin a bit deeper.

If we say that we are not sinners, we are in denial and don't really have the truth within us (1 John 1:8). We know that we sin every day. Though the reader may be a Christian, Christians are not perfect; they do stumble and sin. So, how do we understand this line that is somehow crossed and places the sinner in an eternity without God and outside of heaven? This same Epistle of 1 John helps us answer this question. In context, John uses the word commit or committeth three times in this little epistle in chapter 3, verses 4, 8, and 9. All three uses are the same word (poieo: to commit and continue without delay; "abide" in a negative sense). All three uses indicate that these people are committed to these vices and are practicing them continually.[48] John is referring to the concept of repeating a sin to the point of abandonment. The sins, or vices, listed above are done to the degree that these people put these actions above all else in life. They are totally given over to them.

To counter the idea of being committed to a lifestyle of sin, John uses the term "abide" (meno: to stay in a given place, dwell and endure) twelve times in this book. Again, in context, (verses 2:6, 10, 14, 17, 24, 27 [two times], 28, 3:6, 14, 15, 24) this word is pressing forward the idea that the person who is "abiding" in Christ is someone who is remaining in Him, has an inward sense of communion and relation with Him, and is being anointed by Him continually as His personal possession.[49] This person has fellowship and is permanently living with the Lord Jesus Christ though he is still walking the earth. Though we may on occasion sin, we are no longer committed to sin and, with the help of the Holy Spirit (1 John 4:13), we now live constantly with Him to serve Him and others (1 John 1:7, 2:3, 4:21). Abandoning a life of sin and godlessness, we are now living a life with and for Him.

Let's make some final observations of these above-listed sins. Notice that the first four sins on the list—adultery, fornication, uncleanness, and lasciviousness—are against the seventh commandment (Exodus 20:14)[50]. Again, they display the advanced and abandoned nature of the sinner's life at this stage. Paul calls sexual sins the only sins that a person takes into their very own body (1 Corinthians 6:18). We are to stay away from sexual sins! Idolatry and witchcraft directly violate the first and second commandments as a person places little gods before the One True God (Exodus 20:3-4). We sin against the second commandment of Jesus Christ when we sin against our neighbors with hatred, variance, emulations, wrath, strife, seditions, heresies, envyings, and murders (Matthew 22:39). Lastly, drunkenness and revellings can be classified as sins against ourselves as we combine so many of these sins that are listed here and are completely lost to the godlessness within them.

# 6: GOD'S ACCOUNTING OF LEPERS

S
o far, we've looked at the Luke 17 account where we read of the ten lepers. We've looked at how physically wicked the disease can be, along with how it is considered a spiritual disease in the Bible. Looking at how the Bible also equates it to sin, we then looked at how the disease runs rampant when compared to sin. As a reminder, Leviticus chapter 13 is the account of how the priests were to diagnose and handle leprosy; Leviticus 14 explained how to cure leprosy. These two chapters are keys to understanding how and why lepers were treated as they were in both the Old and New Testaments. Now let's bring in other accounts of lepers as their personal situations are described throughout the Bible. This will enrich the reader's understanding of just how physically and spiritually devastating this disease was, clearly showing the moral breakdown of those who had it and the repentance of those who were cleansed from it. We will look at these sequentially through the Bible in order to save you some page-turning. Additionally, some accounts are evidently parallel accounts, one book to another, so we will cover these accounts as one.

## MOSES' LEPROUS HAND
*Exodus 4:1-9*

God tells Moses that He is going to bring the Israelites out of Egypt and that He will do it in a mighty and obvious way. Moses, on the other hand, tells God that no one will believe that he has seen God. So, God starts to show Moses the amazing things He will do, like turning a rod into a snake and then teaching Moses how to handle that snake. God reminds Moses that He did the same types of things with his ancestors Abraham, Isaac, and Jacob. God directs Moses to put his hand into the chest of his overcoat and, when he removes it, Moses' hand is leprous as God reveals how these miracles will be used to lead the Israelites out of Egypt (vs. 6). God then states in verse 9 that, if the Egyptians do not believe the miracle of the snake or accept that God will make them lepers, the sign that they are full of sin, He will visit many other plagues upon them and their land. God showed Moses that He could give leprosy, the scourge of its day especially in Egypt,[51] and He could cure it. Moses and the Egyptians knew that there was no cure for leprosy. In short, God was physically showing Moses that He was about to demonstrate for Egypt that they were full of sin and that God could do anything He needed to do with this leprous Egyptian people in order to make them set the people of Israel—the apple of God's eye—free (Genesis 12:3, Deuteronomy 32:10, Zechariah 2:8). Who knows? It might be that the Egyptians could have gotten saved, too!

## THE REQUIRED PURITY OF AARON & THE LEVITES
*Leviticus 22:1-6*

In the book of Leviticus, God is relaying the law of the people of Israel to Moses. In this specific passage, the priestly Levites, Aaron's sons of all generations, must separate themselves from all unholy things in life so that they can remain holy for God's personal work amongst the Israelites. If any are found to be unclean, their souls shall be cut off from God. That looks like a reference to eternity. In verse 6, Moses is told that anyone who is a leper cannot touch holy things until he is cured. None of Aaron's offspring could be a leper and be a priest too.

This had to be a devastating blow to Moses, and later would be to Aaron, except for the wonderful news they had just received according to Leviticus chapter 14. God had made a way for them to have leprosy cured. Nothing like this had ever occurred for the leper. Leprosy is clearly being called "unclean," but God gives them a way out of this "sin scourge," a sign of the salvation that was to come into the world in the person of Jesus Christ some 1,500 years later. God provided a way for the spiritual leper. In the meantime, all Levitical priests needed to remember that they were to stay away from sin that could cause the punishment of leprosy..

## KEEP LEPROSY OUT OF THE CAMP
*Numbers 5:1-4*

Again, the Israelites are told that leprosy is defilement, and the leper is not to be around "healthy" people. Putting all lepers, men and women, out of the camp reinforced the punishment and horror placed upon those with leprosy. The observers, those who did not have leprosy and were watching these lepers from afar, wanted nothing to do with them. They did not want to be thrown out of camp and separated from their families. Even with a cure in place, the unsightly illness was treated with the strictest separation. The message for the Israelite was clear. Stay away from sin! "Be holy, for I am holy" (Leviticus11:44-45).

## MIRIAM'S REBELLION & LEPROSY
*Numbers 12:1-16*

God does not like rebellion against Him or His designated leaders. In fact, when His people rebel, He is forced to handle them in some significant and severe way. This is what happened when Miriam, Moses' sister and prophetess of God, and Aaron, Moses' brother and Levitical high priest, spoke against Moses by questioning whether he was really placed in charge by God.

Miriam seems to have been the ringleader when it came to speaking against Moses' leadership.[52] In verse eight, God backs up Moses' leadership and informs Miriam and Aaron that they should have been afraid to speak against Moses. In verse nine, God is angry, and in verse ten, Miriam is made leprous—only Miriam. Aaron admits that both he and Miriam sinned and were foolish, but Moses is the one who prays for her healing. God hears Moses and heals Miriam, but God has her stay outside the camp for seven days: the cleansing verification time for the healing of leprosy (Leviticus 14:9).

God clearly appoints leaders and expects other men to respect them in their position (Romans 13:1-5), even if they are not especially good leaders. David saw that King Saul was not a good leader, but David would not allow anyone to harm a hair on Saul's head and, if Saul was harmed, that man was to be punished (2 Samuel 1:10-16). In our case from Exodus, Moses was God's chosen leader. For Miriam to lead her brother to rebel against and question Moses' authority, God was forced to punish her with leprosy, thus representing the serious sin of rebellion she had just committed. God states that the sin of rebellion is as the sin of witchcraft (1 Samuel 15:23). Miriam had evidently mesmerized herself into thinking that she was equal to or better than Moses. One might take a minute to go back to chapter five of this book and re-read the write-up regarding witchcraft.

## MOSES' FINAL REVIEW OF THE LEPROSY LAWS
*Deuteronomy 24:8*

Moses' final speech before his death on Mount Nebo in Moab (Deuteronomy 34:1-5) includes a warning about leprosy (Deuteronomy 24:8). The topic of leprosy has now taken a significant portion of space in the law given throughout the books of Exodus, Leviticus, Numbers, and Deuteronomy. It was a serious topic, and it took a final comment from Moses to let the Israelites know that it must be handled by the methods described within the law. They were to observe the proper ways to deal with it. Diagnosis, isolation, and treatment—"the cure"—must be done by the book. We are to live by the Lord's commands in His book, or we become spiritual lepers.

## JOAB'S DESCENDANTS
*2 Samuel 3:29*

Abner was a man who was aligned with the house of King Saul, Israel's first earthly king, who was later an enemy of David. David, the future king, and Saul, the present king, were at war and had been for several years. When Abner pulled off an underhanded murder of several of David's right-hand generals within his army, enmity grew even worse. When the war finally did end after King Saul's death, David and Abner made a truce, and David sent Abner home. Peace was declared. Joab, the head of David's army, did not like the truce. He followed Abner and speared Abner to death. David heard about the murder of retaliation and cursed at least one of Joab's descendants in every generation with everything from "issues" (leprosy, crippling defects, and suicide) to hunger (2 Samuel 3:29).

David's handling of Joab involving a warning that included leprosy (and just about everything else that could not be cured in those times) meant that God's vengeance was now upon Joab. David did not go after Joab. He allowed God to take His own rightful role of avenger

(Deuteronomy 32:35, Romans 12:19). Weaker men would want to take vengeance into their own hands. Again, Joab and his descendants knew that leprosy was of God. Joab's sinful vengeance created physical and spiritual leprosy within his own family.

## THE LEPROSY OF NAAMAN, THE SYRIAN CAPTAIN
*2 Kings 5*

The Old Testament is to be used by the New Testament Christian in many ways: history, an account of sacrificial and spiritual laws, wisdom, prophecy, and more (1 Corinthians 10:6, 11, and Jude 7). One extraordinary way that the Old Testament is used by us is for examples of spiritual lessons and personal corrections. The story of Naaman, the captain of the host of the King of Syria, being a leper is one of these wonderful examples.

As the Lord allowed the army of the Syrians to gain power over the northern country of Israel and specifically Samaria, Naaman was used to bring the region under submission. The problem was that Naaman was not only a foreigner, but also a leper. A young, captive Israelite girl who worked in Naaman's house relayed information that it was too bad that he did not get to know a very influential prophet in Samaria named Elisha, for the prophet would have cured Naaman.

When the king of Syria got wind of a possible cure for Naaman, he immediately arranged the trip, the funding, and letters of introduction to have Naaman meet the prophet. The king of Israel, an ungodly man, was none too happy about being placed in the position of supplying a cure to a Syrian. He viewed it as the Syrian king picking a fight if the cure was not forthcoming. Elisha, after hearing that the Israelite king had responded by rending his clothes—a sign of anger and judgment against the Syrian king, sent a message to the Israelite king telling him, essentially, not to worry and simply "let him come to me" (vs. 8).

Elisha was on a mission to show both locals and foreigners that the God of Israel was the only true God.

Naaman became a tad angry when he arrived; Elisha simply relayed a message to him without talking with him face to face, though Naaman was standing right outside Elisha's home. Not only that, but Naaman was told to take seven baths in the Jordan River to be cleansed of leprosy, making him upset all over again! Naaman figured that he could have done that back in Damascus where the rivers were cleaner. But, Naaman was talked into doing this simple, menial task anyway and was healed.

After he had been cured, he immediately travelled back to see Elisha, confirming to Elisha that Naaman now knew that there was only one God on all the earth. He offered Elisha a blessing of coin and exquisite clothing as thanks. Elisha took nothing. Naaman then requested and was granted the amount of earth that two mules could carry so that he, Naaman, could sacrifice to the Lord on the "ground of Israel" within his home country.

The interesting side-note in this story is that Elisha's servant, Gehazi, slipped after Naaman as he was traveling away and begged for some of the coin and clothes that Elisha had rejected. Naaman gave them to him with his blessings, and Gehazi hid the loot at home. As it turned out, Elisha learned of that little move on Gehazi's part by the Lord Himself. When questioned, Gehazi lied that he has gone nowhere when Elisha confronted him with this knowledge. Elisha informed him that he knew all about it and gave Gehazi the leprosy that had just been taken from Naaman. Not only that, but Elisha also gave leprosy to Gehazi's descendants, who would be cursed with leprosy forever.

There is a biblical principle here that we will take a moment to discuss. We, as humans, might be tempted to question why God allowed Gehazi's descendants to receive leprosy. They hadn't done anything wrong—especially if they hadn't yet been born, correct? In other words, why would the "sins of the father" curse the son or his descendants? The principle is found in the chapter that has the Ten Commandments related to us: Exodus 20. In the second commandment, the Word tells us to make no graven images, or, really, no images of any kind (Exodus 20:4). Verse 5 then makes it clear that we should not bow down to any images that might be fashioned before us. And if we do, God states that He is a jealous God and will visit our sins to the third and fourth generations of them that hate Him. This same warning where a father's actions can affect three and four generations is placed in other verses, too: Exodus 34:7, Numbers 14:18, and Deuteronomy 5:9.

We must understand that what we do as parents affects our children. They watch us and imitate our actions. If we go to church and show them that we are sincere Christians, it is a high likelihood that they, too, will become sincere Christians. This effect can go on in a positive fashion for several generations. But, if we show our children a lifestyle that is steeped in sin, a spiritually leprous lifestyle, our children will most likely take this life of sin to themselves, as well. It is easily seen in addictions like gambling, alcohol, drugs, and sex. When a father drinks alcohol even moderately, it is the norm for his children to do so, too. If he is susceptible to being an addict, his children probably will be as well. Thus, the effect of one man's sins can be relayed to following generations if the cycle is not broken. We must view drugs, sex, and all other perversions the same way. If we participate in these sins, there is the highest probability that our children will do likewise.

The Word makes it clear, though, that it does not have to be this way. The Lord asks Ezekiel a question in Ezekiel chapter 18. In verse 2, He asks why Israel uses a proverb that states, "The fathers have eaten sour grapes, and the children's teeth are set on edge." Before Ezekiel can give an answer, the Lord answers His own question by saying that this proverb is no longer going to have occasion to be used. Verses 4 through 18 essentially give the following two messages: 1) the person who commits any of a number of sins listed shall die for his own sins. But, if a person who is the son of this sinning father does not take up his father's sins, but instead lives a righteous life, this son shall not bear the iniquities of his father (vs. 19 and 20). 2) God adds to this precept by saying that the father who lives a righteous life, though his son does not, will not suffer the sins of his son upon himself.

Here is the bottom line. Verse 21 states that if a man will turn from his sin and keep God's commands and statutes and live a righteous life, he shall live. The righteous man shall not die in his sins. Verse 27 states clearly that this man who has corrected his life "shall save his soul alive." This is living a repentant life. This idea of repentance is reinforced one more time at the end of this chapter. Verse 31 tells us to throw all of our transgressions out and make a new heart and spirit, thus asking ourselves, "Why should we die?" There is no reason to die in these sins from which we've not repented. Verse 32 caps the whole idea that we are able to turn our lives around. It states, "For I have no pleasure in the death of him that dieth, saith the Lord God: wherefore turn yourselves, and live ye."

If we choose not to turn away from our sins, there is nothing God can do for us. It is our own choice to live a life of spiritual leprosy. He doesn't like the fact that we will not choose Him, but only asks that we turn, another word for "repent," and live for Him. In so doing, we don't set the teeth of our children on edge by relaying an ungodly lifestyle to them. Instead, we give them a godly example of life that doesn't create for them a lifestyle that they must overcome. We are now responsible for our own lives. Our example in life does matter to our children. The spiritual lesson that we learn from Gehazi's actions is that he is the person who caused spiritual leprosy to be conveyed to his following generations. He made a very bad choice with regard to himself and his family.

Now, knowing the story, here are some interesting teaching points. Naaman is a foreigner—what we would call a Gentile. He is cursed with the scourge of leprosy and is in need of salvation from this scourge viewed as sin. The missionary, a young, captive Israelite girl, tells him how he can find the cure—salvation—from a prophet she's heard of. The king, sparing neither time nor expense, sends him on a mission with his written commendation and all of the wealth needed to procure such a healing. When he arrives at Elisha's doorstep, a representation of Jesus Christ in the Old Testament, Elisha doesn't even see him face to face, but gives him "the Word of Salvation"—the cure. Naaman, irritated that Elisha didn't even come out to see him, thinking that this is too easy and that it can't be a real salvation, at first rejects the Word of salvation and starts to turn away. He is stopped by friends who reiterate to him that salvation may not be that hard. Had it been hard, Elisha would have directed him to go "that route." Following through with the simple steps of cleansing, Naaman is washed clean. He tries to pay for the salvation, but salvation is free, and, this time, Elisha even talks with him lovingly face to face.

Let's say all of this in another way. Naaman hears of salvation, though he did not even understand that it was there for the taking. He had previously been in the land of God, but had not understood that salvation was at hand. Though he had left the land, the Lord gave him reason to return to the kingdom for salvation. We don't seek God, but He does seek us as we are assisted by some "missionary of the world" and are aided, even unknowingly, by friends who arrange for us to be at the right place and in the right time, helping us with their wealth of knowledge and assistance. When we are led by the Lord to be saved, we don't talk with Him face to face but are introduced to Him through the Word of the Bible. Salvation is a free gift to us, not of works or payments, so that no man can boast on what he did for his own salvation (Ephesians 2:8-9).

When we are cleansed and still find that we cannot pay for the gift of salvation, we go our way, wanting a piece of our new home to go with us wherever we go, giving glory and credit to God for our salvation. Our desire is to live a life of sacrifice and service to the Lord. Suddenly, wherever we are is a piece of home, even though we are now aliens in an alien land. When we meet a person we truly believe to be a brother or sister, we give of our bounty without question, knowing that the "Gehazis" in our lives either will take the gift and use it wisely or will take the gift under less-than-honorable pretense, and God will deal with them.

Well, God dealt with Gehazi. Gehazi and his descendants would be given leprosy. His sin of greed gave him worldly wealth, as there is no indication that the wealth was given back. But, his wealth did him no good when he was most assuredly ejected outside the city walls or limits as a pauper. The Word records no apologies or repentance offered by Gehazi to Elisha. He didn't offer to take the gifts back to Naaman. We are lead to believe that Gehazi was given to sin, and, in sin, he was scourged with leprosy. Naaman received the reward of salvation, while Gehazi was cursed with leprosy.

Stories of people who have pretended to be followers of Christ are today too frequent. Their arrogance—seeking "health, wealth, and happiness" without the right hearts—is a disaster-in-the-making. Jesus never promised us lives without trials, only that we can have peace in Him as we do His work (John 16:33). With His power, we overcome adversity, though we may not become wealthy in the worldly sense.

## THE FOUR LEPERS OF OPPORTUNITY
*2 Kings 7*

The Israelite city of Samaria is being destroyed by the invading Syrians—or at least the Syrians are attempting to take the city. Obviously, all supplies to the Samarians have been cut off. The Samarians are hungry (vs. 12). The Syrians have a massive siege camp outside, with every soldier simply awaiting the fall of Samaria (vs. 5). But, the Lord has made the Syrians hear what they believe to be a great noise of Hittite and Egyptian chariots, armies they think may have been hired by the Samarians to take the Syrians out. Such was not the case, but the armies of the Syrians believe it is and flee their camp and head for home, abandoning a fully-stocked and wealthy camp. While precious food is selling for abnormally high prices inside the Samarian city, all the food one might want is sitting outside the gates of the city in the camp of the Syrians.

With the stage set, we can now listen to a conversation that occurs between Elisha the prophet and a lord upon which the king over Samaria relies heavily (vs. 1-2). Elisha announces that, by "tomorrow about this time," the price of food within the city of Samaria is going to be at relatively low prices. With no hope in sight for the people of the city, this was an astonishing declaration. Now, even though Elisha is a reliable prophet and has repeatedly proven to receive messages from God, this lord quips that "if the Lord would make windows in heaven, might this thing be?" The "little lord" has just shown his lack of faith by saying that even if God could see through windows from heaven, God couldn't arrange for this to be done; the little lord doesn't believe that God is watching, but if He was, He couldn't make the price of food come down. Elisha's answer ought to have chilled the lord's bones. Elisha prophesied that he will see it, but will not eat of the food.

Meanwhile, the story's focus moves to four lepers who are discussing where they are going to die. Remember that lepers are not to be in the city (Leviticus 13:46), yet here they are preparing to enter the city (vs. 3). They debate the wisdom of going into the city, which is their only present hope of food to prevent their death by starvation, knowing that little food will be available there. Secondly, no one will share food with a leper who is already cursed to die a miserable death. Who knows but that the city's inhabitants might simply kill them for the crime of entering the city! No matter which option they take, they expect to die.

Then, in verse 4, they realize that the option of entering the Syrian camp exists, and it may have possible "better results" for them. They know the Syrians have food. They know that they might kill them just for being "enemy lepers!" But, they also know there's a chance that the Syrians could spare their lives, thus guaranteeing them some good food and an extension on life. So, early in the morning, they enter the Syrian camp at the most distant point from the city. Shocked to find no one there, they find the food and enjoy the best meal they've had in a long time. After their appetites are satisfied, they start carrying away the gold and silver that they find, hiding it for later use.

The lepers realize that the time will come when the Samarians find out about the camp's abandonment, and then they, themselves, will be found out. Understanding that it's better to be on the "informing end," they report the news to a city official who then tells the king. The truth is verified, and the city of Samaria is freed to buy food. All's well that ends well, except for the lord we first talked about. He sees the food selling for low costs and tries to guide the people from the city into the camp in an organized fashion, but he is trampled to death in the ensuing rush for food. Thus, Elisha's prophecy is fulfilled that the lord would see it with his own eyes but not eat of it.

In this story, the lepers start out on a mission to create their own "salvation." They were not welcome in the city and might have been killed for entering it. Either way, their leprous condition guaranteed them death sooner or later. By deciding to enter the Syrian camp, they make the startling discovery that it is empty of people and well-stocked with food and wealth. Even as leprous as they are in their "sinful condition," they choose to do the right thing, telling the city of the situation. They've found great riches, salvation, and nourishment, and have turned their hearts around by informing others of the wealth to be found there. They were, in New Testament terms, a picture of the unrighteous stumbling on a wealth that keeps them alive. They were saved, but the lord did not believe and was trampled to death by those who rushed to find the plentiful salvation about which they had been told. Spiritual lepers can find the greatest wealth in salvation and food for their souls. It's their choice to search for it.

## KING AZARIAH'S LEPROSY
*2 Kings 15:1-6*

Leaders are expected to do that which God values and to act in ways in which He directs them. This is the case in this short account of King Azariah, king of the southern kingdom of Judah. Azariah, the son of a godly king named "Amaziah," also did right in God's eyes, just as his father had done (vs. 3). Verse 4 is the key in this passage. It starts with the phrase, "Save that ...." According to the passage, all that King Azariah did during his fifty-two year reign was good with God, save that he did not take down the idolatrous "high places" where the people of Judah offered ungodly sacrifices and burnt incense to their lesser gods.

As king and spiritual leader of the people of Judah, Azariah was duty-bound to try at the least to get the people to follow the One True God who led them out of their captivity of Egypt. If the king's leadership skills were poor and he failed to accomplish this re-focus to the God of the Israelites, he could at least point to the fact that he had tried. If he had even taken it to the next and proper step of asking God for His assistance to get the job done, we can readily believe that God would have made him successful. Though he was a good man in God's eyes, God viewed his overall leadership or kingship as a failure. Obviously, God expected more.

The Lord "smote" him with leprosy due to his failure in leadership. Jesus tells the parable of the servant who was not doing that which was proper while he awaited the Lord's return, and the Lord finds him not doing the required work (Luke 12:48). He informs the man that he had been given much (we might call it wealth and talent), and that it had been expected of him to do a great deal of good work with it. The servant did not. So, the man is beaten with many "stripes," scourged for not working as he should. Paul states that a steward, a person placed in charge of his Lord's goods, is to be faithful as he will be judged for his work (1 Corinthians 4:2-3).

King Azariah, shown as an example for us, can be termed the "steward" of his kingdom for the Lord. At some point in time, the Lord must have determined that he had not and would not correct this situation of idolatry within the kingdom. The result was that the king was punished with leprosy and would live the remainder of his days as a leper, having placed his son—who was not ready to be king—in charge of the kingdom. We must realize that, when we come to Christ and know the work that we ought to be doing, we must take hold of it and get it done. If we don't, we place undue burden on others and become the spiritual leper being chastised by God.

Does this mean that the saved aren't saved, or that they can lose their salvation? No. The Bible praises King Azariah in everything but his failure in this task. God chastises us and supplies consequences to us when we are not faithful to the work assigned to us. For us, we do not lose our salvation, but we can lose crowns or rewards earned for the service we once performed for Him when we are not faithful to the work before us (1 Corinthians 3:13-15). King Azariah was a believer in the Holy One of Israel, but his reputation was marred with spiritual leprosy when he did not perform the work that was clearly his to attempt to complete. Failing in specific work that God has assigned us, we are ushered into heaven just as if we passed through fire getting there, all of our works of hay and stubble being burned to ashes.

## KING UZZIAH'S LEPROSY
*2 Chronicles 26*

Pride and our image of "self-perfection" can create a spirit of arrogance that invades our life and overshadows the things we've done in life. King Uzziah is an excellent example of this "about face." We are told in verse four that he did that which was right in the eyes of God. He sought God, and God made him prosper because of it (vs. 5). He made war against the enemies of God. He strengthened the walls and protection of the great city of Jerusalem. He helped the surrounding area by digging wells, protecting the locals with outpost towers, and helping the farmers with their vine dressing. His army was large, powerful, well outfitted, and well led. He even built great war machines that could launch arrows and large stones from the city to protect itself. He was a good and active king.

But, in verse 16, we are informed that his pride got the better of him. He went into the temple and usurped the role of priest by burning incense on the altar. The temple priest whose name was Azariah informed him that he shouldn't be doing that and that it would go "bad" for him. King Uzziah was angered by Azariah's comment. As he stood there with the censer in his hand, leprosy rose up in his forehead, and he was cast out of the temple and into a separated house to live the remainder of his days. It states that he "was cut off from the house of the Lord" and his son—who was not ready for kingship—ruled in his stead (vs. 21), repeating the history of King Azariah and his own son.

Pride is one of those sins we could have added to the Galatians 5:19-21 study in chapter 5, placing it in the "Such Like" category. We become better in our own eyes than we really are. We believe ourselves to be a "legend in our own mind." We start to think that our strength comes from our own power, forgetting that God is the one who allowed us to be strong and successful. We become wise in our own eyes (Proverbs 3:7). Instead, we are to see ourselves as lowly, lower than other men, having unity with them and not being wise in our own pride (Romans 12:16). King Uzziah ruined his own testimony by assuming a role that was not his and that he was not ordained to perform: a priest. We need to remember to work for the Lord within our gifts and talents, not thinking ourselves greater than we are. Or, we too shall become spiritual lepers.

## JESUS' TESTIMONY FOR JOHN THE BAPTIST
*Matthew 11*

John the Baptist sends a message to Jesus Christ, asking if Jesus is "He that should come" (vs. 3). Christ sends word back to John the Baptist stating that great works are being done. John the Baptist is evidently questioning—or being questioned by his disciples—whether Jesus is the Messiah (vs. 2-3). Jesus is very clear. This chapter in Matthew is dedicated not only to showing the wonderful works of Christ but also to showing that many people and cities will have seen these works, will have rejected Jesus Christ, and will suffer because of this rejection during the coming day of judgment (vs. 5, 6, 21-24). Matthew gives a glowing testimony to the work of John the Baptist in that he was a strong messenger and precursor for Christ (vs. 7-19). Regardless of what people choose to think of John, Jesus stated here that John has done the work he was to complete and that people who accept John's work and the work of Christ are wise (vs. 14, 19, 25-30).

For our specific purposes with respect to leprosy, verse 5 is a testimony to the work of Christ and is a list of work that John would recognize as works of the Messiah. No one in the Old Testament received the gift of sight, yet in the New Testament, we see that Jesus Christ gave the gift of sight frequently. This gift of sight that Jesus gave to the people of His day also partially fulfills the prophecy of Isaiah 35:5, which is a millennial age prophecy. This passage fully fulfills the prophecy in Isaiah 61:1 in the preaching of the gospel. The fact that lepers are not only cured but also cleansed shows that God is at work here. All of these miracles, including the deaf having hearing restored and the dead being raised up, were amazing things to see, and they testified that the Messiah was at hand. Not only that, Jesus added in verse 6 that anyone who accepts these things is blessed. We are not to be offended by Jesus Christ and His work. In fact, it is clear that He will not stand for us in the day of judgment if we do not stand for Him and confess Him before men while we are walking here on earth (Matthew 10:32-33). Jesus was doing away with the spiritual leper for anyone who would accept Him.

## JESUS VISITS SIMON THE LEPER
*Matthew 26:1-16*

Jesus' visit at the house of Simon the leper is covered twice, once in Matthew 26:6 and once in Mark 14:3. We'll use the Matthew passage as our text. Jesus is near the end of His earthly three-year ministry. He has stated that two days from now, during the Feast of the Passover, He will be betrayed and crucified (vs. 1). Details of the discussion that the chief priests, scribes, and elders had with Caiaphas, the high priest, on their plans to capture Jesus and kill Him are given here to us (vs. 3-5). This chapter also details the circumstances of the betrayal agreement between Judas Iscariot and the chief priests (vs. 14-16).

During these discussions, Jesus is at the house of a man called "Simon the Leper" (vs. 6) in Bethany. The account includes a woman with an alabaster box that contains a very precious ointment, which she pours over His head as He sits at the table having a meal with his disciples (vs. 7). The disciples are annoyed that such expensive ointment is wasted for such a purpose when it could have been sold and the money given to the poor, but Jesus calls it a good work, saying that it is done for His burial, that what she has done will forever be remembered, and that it will be a memorial to her (vs. 8-13).

The comment we are interested in for our study is the one that reveals that Jesus was in the house of Simon the leper. Since Jesus and so many other people are at this house for this meal, we can assume that Simon is no longer a leper. Otherwise, he would not have a house where others were visiting—unless it was possibly a shack where he could get out of the weather. Additionally, Jesus was quite likely the one who would have cleansed him, with a lesser possibility that one of His Apostles may have done it in the name of Jesus Christ. Either way, it makes sense that Simon must have been at the home for the meal and had been, therefore, previously cleansed.

Think back on all of the accounts involving lepers that were healed. Notice that the Word does not describe what the leper looks like other than having the individual leper's skin restored to health. For example, Naaman's healing from leprosy clearly states that his skin became like that of a little child after the healing (2 Kings 5:14). In the Luke 17 passage discussing our ten lepers, all were mobile, and the one clearly was able to return and give worship to Jesus Christ. We never really know that all of their physical maladies associated with leprosy were corrected, but we're going to make the assumption that Jesus did nothing "half way." He would not have left the crippling affects unchanged and the skin restored. He had the power to completely restore, and it is believed that this is what He did. These were fully restored people.

We can also believe that Simon has been fully restored and is sitting at a meal, dining with his Messiah. Simon has fellowship with Jesus, His disciples, and clearly with other friends like the lady with the ointment. This is likely Mary of Bethany whose same account of anointing with the expensive ointment is given in John 12:1-3, except that no mention is made of the leper, and the time line is a few days different. Even Lazarus, whom Jesus raised from the dead, is said to be at the table in the account in the Gospel of John. Again, the point is that Simon's life has been fully restored to him. Though he is called "the leper," it has become more of a badge of honor and testimony for Simon. No after-effects are present. He is no longer a leper.

The same can be said for the spiritual ex-leper of today. Though we were once a people in bondage to sin and were infected with deadly and sinful maladies that would one day kill us for eternity, as Christians we are now presentable to Jesus Christ and His Father. We have the Holy Spirit residing within us. We have been forgiven, and the leprosy has been removed. As a side note, if you are not a Christian, we will be discussing the solution shortly. There is hope for you!

## A LEPER HEALED BY THE TOUCH OF JESUS CHRIST
*Mark 1:40-45*

The three accounts of a man who had leprosy, was touched by Jesus Christ, and was healed, appear to be the same event recorded by these three disciples. All three occur early in Christ's ministry, and all three are nearly identical in language and account. For our purposes, we are going to look at them all as the same account. We will use Mark 1:40-45 as the main account, but one can read the other two accounts, located in Matthew 8:1-4 and in Luke 5:12-15.

The account opens with the leper approaching Jesus and "beseeching" (parakaleo: to desire, entreat, pray) Him (vs. 40). This person was imploring Christ and asking Him to do a great thing for him. He kneels before Christ, an act of worship, and tells Christ that, if He wills it, He can make him clean. This wasn't asked from a view towards healing, but of being cleansed. This statement reinforces the idea that leprosy was a punishment placed on a victim for their sin, of which they needed to be cleansed. Remember that in the Jewish knowledge of Scripture, only God could cleanse leprosy.

Jesus is moved with compassion (splagchnizomai: sympathy or pity) for the leper and reaches His hand out to touch him. Jesus makes it clear that it certainly is His will and that He commands it to be done, by two simple words in the Greek.[53] Immediately, as soon as Christ spoke the words, the man was cleansed and the leprosy had departed. Here is the interesting part of the account. Jesus charges him not to tell anyone what has happened! He is to go and present himself to the priests and to do what the law of Moses had directed, "for a testimony to them" (vs. 44).

Let's first consider verse 45 and then discuss this comment that Jesus Christ made. In verse 45, we learn that the leper can't hold the miracle in and "publishes" it abroad. The news of the miracle creates such a sensation that Christ has to move elsewhere to continue His ministry.

Again, this is early in the earthly ministry of Jesus. These miracles that He is doing "right out of the gate" are an amazing experience for those who witness them. He is curing diseases and casting out devils (vs. 34). He has already healed Simon Peter's mother (vs. 30-31). And now He cures a leper, work that only God can do. This creates a blaze (vs. 45) that brings people from all quarters to Christ for healing and perhaps simply to see this Man of God preach and heal.

But, Christ's command to say nothing but simply to go and show his cleansing to the priest likely was not because Christ did not want notoriety. Instead, it was to fulfill two needs. First, the law in Leviticus was clear that one had to show his or her cleansing to the priest in order to be certified clean and receive approval to reenter society. Christ was not trying to keep the law in place as much as fulfilling rules and regulations that were presently in place.

The second reason, though, is more assuredly the deeper reason that Christ wanted the ex-leper to go to the priest first. This "certification of cleansing" was to be a testimony to the priests and thus to all Israel.

They knew the facts surrounding a cleansing of leprosy. They knew that God was the "performer" of this miracle. This was at the beginning of Jesus' ministry, and it's likely that He wanted them to know that the Messiah, God walking the earth in Jesus Christ, was here performing the impossible. He wanted the priests to wake up and realize that all of God's Israelites were seeing the dawn of the Messianic age.

But, it didn't work. Did the ex-leper tell the priestly authorities? Since Christ commanded him to do so, it's a reasonably good assumption that he did. Even if he did not, there would now be enough lepers coming before the priests for certification of cleansing that the news on the street had to be shouted. "The Messiah is here!" The contrary is more easily believed. The priests in the temple of Jerusalem did not want people to believe that "The Christ" was on the scene. They were already rejecting Him because they could see the end of their "priestly jobs" if the Messiah was here. In their understanding, the advent of the Messiah meant that sacrifice and the temple were no longer needed. With God the Messiah taking His rightful place here on earth, they as priests were no longer needed. They didn't want to lose their power and dominance over the people of Israel. They didn't want to stop receiving the tithes and offerings.

From Christ's vantage point, He wanted a shout of acclamation to go up throughout the land, one that would make every knee bow to Him; the start of the Messianic age could begin. If they would but accept Him, they would have the promised godly King that would rule in righteousness and peace (Isaiah 2:2-4). But, repeated accounts throughout and even after His earthly ministry showed that Israel did not want the Messiah. The nation simply wanted another earthly king whom they could manipulate and who would destroy the power that Rome had over them, thus leaving them in power and unaccountable to God.

Before discussion on this passage is closed, let's take some time to look at my statement above that intimates that Christ would have started His earthly rule if only Israel had accepted Him as the Messiah. Many Scriptures in the Old Testament assure us that Israel's proper role would be that of being missionaries to the world of the Gentiles—all nationalities that were not Israelites. In addition to the above-stated verse of Isaiah 2:2-4, one can read a few of the verses where they were assigned this missionary work in Psalm 72 and 96, Isaiah 52:7-15, and Isaiah Chapters 60 and 62. All the Israelites would have needed to do was accept Him, and the Messianic Age would have been ushered into effect. But, as so many other verses indicate, this was not prophesied to occur.

Jesus even states this in Matthew 23:34-39. He has wanted to gather them to Himself, as a hen gathers her chicks, but, as they have killed the prophets, they will continue to kill them in the future. He even alludes to His own crucifixion in verse 34. In verse 37, He reiterates that they would not accept Him. Instead, they reject Him, and their house is made desolate (verses 38 and 39). They will not see Him again until He comes in the name of the Lord at the end of the Great Tribulation (Revelation 19:11-16). By the way, this account, given in Matthew 23, is three days before He is crucified. He knows that they have already rejected Him.

This is not the only indication of rejection, though. In Isaiah 53:8, He is also cut off from the land of the living. Daniel indicates as much in Daniel 9:26, where he says, "And after three score and two weeks shall Messiah be cut off, but not for Himself." In Luke 17:25, Jesus states that He must suffer and be rejected by His own generation. At His trial, the Jews cry for Barabbas to be released and for Christ to be taken away, thus rejecting Christ (Luke 23:28). This act of replacement with a murderer is also reflected in the Acts of the Apostles where Luke writes that Christ was rejected (Acts 3:14). In John 1:11, John states that Christ—the Word— came, and His own did not receive Him.

Additional verses indicate the reason that this rejection occurred. In Romans chapters 9, 10, and 11, Paul addresses our answer. The Israelites were to be God's missionaries to the world. In Romans 9:24, we're told that the Jews and the Gentiles have been called to salvation. The Gentiles responded in faith and accepted His call (Romans 9:30), but the Jews responded by denying Him and wanted to stay with the Mosaic Law (Romans 9:31). Grace, not the law, is the only way to salvation (Romans 11:6), and they rejected it and were blinded (Romans 11:7). God is now using the Gentile world population to provoke Israel into wanting a salvation by grace, not law (Romans 11:11). During this "Church Age," God is winning the Gentiles to Himself. The Gentiles do not replace Israel. In other words, the "church" does not replace Israel as the inheritors of Christ's promises.

Instead, we are living in a time of "hiatus" where Israel is not being dealt with by the Lord Jesus Christ except indirectly. There is a time when the Gentiles will have had their "day" on earth, and God will hand it back to the Jews to take up their rightful place in history and be the "People of God." Again in Romans, we learn that Israel will be turned from ungodliness, and their sins will be removed (Romans 11:26-27). The time of the Gentiles will be fulfilled at that point (Romans 11:25). Again, though, this day in time is specifically designed by God and Israel is temporarily made an enemy so that the Gentiles could have a time to come to repentance and salvation (Romans 11:28, 29). Paul, the apostle to the Gentiles, states that this time was needed in order for a Gentile world to be called to Christ, whether they accept this calling or not. Paul states this when he says that he is turning to the Gentiles to win them, as many as would be saved (Acts 13:46-48). God used this time to win Gentiles to the Lord (Acts 14: 27).

To us, it's a bit confusing. Israel, preferably, would have accepted her role as missionaries of the world. To date, the Israelites have not done so. In the future (during the Great Tribulation), they will accept this role. In the meantime, we trust God's methodology without understanding it all yet (Romans 11:33-36). Israel will one day be grafted back into His olive tree again (Romans 11:21-24).

Unknowingly, this leper had provided a vehicle for Christ to examine the hearts of the Israelites. He had worshipped Jesus, kneeling before Him, and even calling Him "Lord" in the Matthew and Luke accounts (Matthew 8:2, Luke 5:12). The common man and sinner knew who Jesus was. The priests could not squelch the news that the Messiah had come. The leper went away free from sin, cleansed, and whole, but the priests were now moving toward a time where they would be the spiritual lepers of the kingdom. In their worldly wisdom, the priests were being made lepers.

## A SCOURGE OF LEPROSY
*Luke 4:16-30*

The Gospel writer, Luke the Evangelist, uses this account to show when Jesus came into public ministry. He comes to Nazareth, His boyhood home town, and goes to the synagogue. This day, He stands to read from the Scriptures and reads Isaiah chapter 61:1-2, for about a verse and a half (Luke 4:16-19). The portion of Scripture that Jesus quoted is a beautiful passage and deserves to be quoted here, as follows:

> *The Spirit of the Lord is upon Me, because He hath anointed Me to preach the gospel to the poor; he hath sent me to heal the brokenhearted, to preach deliverance to the captives, and recovering of sight to the blind, to set at liberty them that are bruised, to preach the acceptable year of the Lord.*

As He finishes and closes the book, handing it down to the minister, He sits down, saying, "This day is this scripture fulfilled in your ears" (vs. 20-21). He proclaimed Himself to be the Messiah. All seem gracious as they watch Him but are shocked at the words that have just come out of His mouth, even questioning His parentage (vs. 22).

Then, Jesus turns up the heat, prophesying that they will one day tell Him to heal Himself and that He should do the miracles He has done elsewhere "here" in Nazareth (vs. 23). He affirms this negative view of theirs when He states that no prophet is accepted in his own country (vs. 24). Jesus recalls the days of Elijah when he had closed up the heavens from rain for three years and only the widow, Sarepta, was cared for with food and oil by Elijah even though there were many widows in Israel (vs. 25-26). Jesus adds one more zinger: that lepers were not cleansed in the time of Elisha, except for Naaman the Syrian, and he was a foreigner, a Gentile (vs. 27). Then the people in the synagogue try to kill Jesus by throwing Him off of a cliff in their anger, but Jesus evades them (vs. 28-30).

Again, within our study, the leper is the focus here. The Israelites had the law, and the book of Leviticus within the law contained the procedures to cleanse lepers of leprosy. But, not one account is given where the cleansing is put into practice, save the accounts of Miriam and Moses, who were special cases. The only account of cleansing was that of Naaman the Syrian. He was the only person who sought the cleansing. Since he was a foreigner, he didn't even have to show himself to the temple priest. Why hadn't other Israelites requested and been granted cleansing? Christ makes it clear that many lepers were in the house of Israel at the time.

Jesus seems to be giving them a challenge to later remember His words as they stood this day in Nazareth. Soon, they would hear of widows being cared for by Him. Soon, they would hear of lepers being cleansed. With this prophecy in their minds, they would remember that He had told them of the events before they happened. Maybe, then they would believe in the Boy-grown-into-a-Man in their midst; Jesus Christ grown up in the little town of Nazareth.

We also need to understand that He is trying to cleanse us from our spiritual leprosy. Let's look at this in chapter 7.

# 7: GOD'S CLEANSING FOR LEPROSY

After looking at the physical and spiritual aspects of leprosy, we've seen how the Word of God equates leprosy spiritually to sin. The picture is neither pretty nor pleasant. This sin is contagious and can now be seen running rampant in today's society, easily observed when we reviewed the Galatians passage in chapter 5. In many ways, the situation may seem bleak or hopeless to the reader. Most of the discussion so far has focused on how we become spiritual lepers. The passages we've seen from the Old Testament show example after example of how people became lepers. Only the example of Naaman relates the true spirit of repentance and the resultant cleansing. These biblical representatives did things that caused serious consequences to themselves and their families. The actions of Miriam, Gehazi, Captain Joab, King Azariah, and King Uzziah reflect the temporary or permanent spirits of rebellion that placed God in the position of having to supply consequences to their actions. Their sins enacted sequences that changed their own lives as well as the present and future lives of their family members. Even the kingdom around them was changed as their own services were removed from society and others were forced to step into roles for which they likely were not ready. Succeeding generations were changed due to their sins.

Sin, and addiction to sin, changes the lives of those who are in bondage to it. They are not able to be the leaders that they were designed to be both within their own families and in society. Maturity was supposed to have grown for each of them throughout their lives in order for them to be more capable and ready to assume higher duties planned for them by God. Their growth is subsequently stunted by their addictions and, therefore, the talents given them will go partly or wholly unused. What a waste.

In essence, the addiction-to-self that such people have creates unproductive lives that engender more unproductive lives in the families, friends, and coworkers with whom they associate. Even if such people do not succumb to the sin to which they are exposed by the spiritual leper, the local community residing around these people is less effective within their areas of influence than they might have been. The talents that the addicts have wasted result in their not being in the right place at the right time. Yes, God will raise up other people to fill in those talents where needed. But, think about what He could have achieved had the addict not been selfish. Two could have stood in the gap, rather than only one.

Dwight L. Moody called these people his "gap men."[54] Ezekiel offers the idea for this, as follows:

> *And I sought for a man among them, that should make up the hedge, and stand in the gap before Me for the land, that I should not destroy it: but I have found none (Ezekiel 22:30).*

These are the mature Christians of today whom we can look to in order to fill the gap (Hebrew perets: the breach or break) and avert calamity.[55] They are to serve in the gap as intercessors of instruction to keep the dam from breaking forth. The Lord tells Ezekiel in this verse that this is the "hedge" (Hebrew gader: enclosure, fence, hedge, wall) to shut off God's judgment by winning people to the Lord. The same idea is put forth in verses such as Genesis 18:26, Psalm 106:23, Isaiah 59:16, Jeremiah 5:1, and Jeremiah 15:1. God is continuing to seek men and women to fill the gap and take the Word to those who need to hear it. When they are not found, it causes the gap and future destruction.

Moody desired to keep people from being destroyed as spiritual lepers both in the short term here on earth and in the long term: eternity. He was looking for Christians to stand in the gap. As Ezekiel is told, though, they are not available or ready to serve in the Lord's army. Mature Christians are necessary but are not found to teach and preach the Word to those who are falling through the gap into the torrent that will overwhelm them for eternity. D. L. Moody's solution was to start a teaching school, which later became The Moody Bible Institute. This was and is a good solution. It has stood in the gap for over 120 years and today still carries on the training of gap men and women for the Lord's work.

Moody's belief, moreover, was that all men do not necessarily need to receive this in-depth education from such an institute in order to be a gap-filler. Yes, this may be the proper route for most of our church pastors and formal "educators," but most Christians can assist in filling this gap simply by getting into the Word. By studying it and hiding it in their hearts by solid Bible study, Christians will be ready to put Scripture forth so that other men can be thoroughly prepared to stand in the gap (2 Timothy 3:15 – 4:2), stopping the flow of souls who are being lost to Satan's realm and efforts.

Paul calls this work the ministry of "reconciliation" in 2 Corinthians 5:17-21. As we are won to Christianity, repenting of our sins and depending upon Jesus Christ's work on the cross for salvation, we become new creations in Christ (vs. 17). We are reconciled to

Him, and now we begin our work of reconciling others to Him as well. "Reconciliation," or the act of reconciling, is an interesting word meaning "restoration to divine favor." It is the reestablishment of a broken relationship.[56] When Adam sinned, the lineage of man had a broken relationship with God. This relationship with God is restored for those who become reconciled to Him.

Paul labels the people who do this work as "ambassadors" in verse 20. These are the people who are elder representatives and preachers for Christ, traveling and working as envoys for Christ. It could be argued that Paul means only for this role to be held by the elders or pastors of a New Testament church. But, notice in verses 19 and 20 that he is including "us" in the work of reconciliation. In other words, Paul is looking for mature Christians who are willing to go out and help their local church and pastor as envoys, those who fill the gap and staunch the outflow of losses to Satan. This isn't a job reserved only for the original apostles or today's pastors in the New Testament church. Everyone has the duty to grow into a mature Christian and fill the gap. We have a duty to stop the advance of spiritual leprosy in our day. Look at how Scripture supplies the answer that corrects the flood of spiritual leprosy.

We are not lost or destitute without a path to correct our spiritual leprosy. We are not without an extended hand to which we can latch onto before we drown in our addictions and sin. Regardless of our spiritually crippling and leprous disfigurement, a disease that has made us totally reprehensible to God, we are loved (John 3:16). Even before the world began, the Triune God looked forward, saw man's need for salvation, and developed a pathway to that salvation because we are loved by Him (2 Timothy 1:9-10, Hebrews 2:3-4).

Many times throughout this book, we've made the statement that the only person who can cure leprosy is God. Even today, both physically and spiritually, this is still true. Yes, man has developed medicines to arrest and stop its physically destructive progress. One day, God willing, man will find a cure that does kill the bacteria within the body, but the cure will not likely reverse leprosy's effects. And then, the cure will actually have come from God anyway. Physical leprosy remains today a hideous and disfiguring ailment when not caught and arrested in its early stages. Only God can cure physical leprosy and reverse the damage it has done to the body.

Our goal in this book is to allow God to come in and cure the ravages and disease that spiritual leprosy has caused within us. He loves us and didn't leave us here without a method of salvation from a life of sin. He has provided a cure for our leprosy.

For a moment, let me step back to cover some thoughts on salvation. It occurs to me that the reader may not be a Christian. You may not have repented of your sins and placed your faith in the Lord's work upon the cross. Maybe you've picked up this book and have become so *enthralled* by it that you've continued reading it! If that is the case, you are most welcome here. So, in the following few pages, I will insert a six-point biblical method for you to use to ask Jesus Christ into your life and, as a result, you can allow the Lord to initiate healing you from your leprosy. After this section, I've included my personal testimony that may help you see the odd and unexpected ways that Christ calls us and works in our lives. For those of you who are already Christians, you may want to skim through this portion of the book and resume your study where the paragraph starts with "Before we leave the specific topic of salvation."

It will take some understanding on the unbelieving reader's part to move to the healing and cleansing of leprosy. In the next Six Points, read to understand and then heed what it takes for the unsaved sinner, the spiritual leper, to be saved and cleansed for eternity:

## POINT ONE

We'll continue to use the Bible as a base or source of the knowledge that leads to this cleansing. In Romans 1:16-17, Paul states that he is not ashamed of the gospel, suggesting that we should not be ashamed of it either. God has this power, this cure, that is His will to see us saved. We have to believe in His work with all of our heart (Acts 8:37) in order for Him to supply righteousness to us so that we can live by faith in Him (Romans 1:17). In short, put your faith in the Word of Jesus Christ, the Holy Bible. Then, you have the basis in which to advance to the next step in the cleansing (2 Peter 1:20-21).

This needs a moment of clarification and reinforcement. We need to realize that Jesus is "The Word." He was the Word even in eternity past (John 1:1). The Father, Jesus, and the Holy Spirit all agree and bear testimony to the truth that Jesus is the way to salvation (1 John 5:5-8). He who believes this truth overcomes the world and receives salvation. John 1:14 states that He was made flesh, born of a woman and made man (Luke 2:11), and came to live with mankind to relay this grace and truth. The confirmation that His name is "The Word of God" occurs in Revelation 19:13. When you read the Bible, you must recognize that these are Jesus' words and they must be believed and heeded. They were written for us in eternity past as God knows all things: past, present, and future (John 21:17, 1 John 3:20). We are to follow His Word.

As we continue with Point One, remember that Naaman did not realize that the road to salvation was really quite easy. He had to be convinced that his cleansing from leprosy was as easy as following the words of the Prophet Elisha. It may be that you will need to read this section several times, along with the Scriptures that accompany my comments, in order to realize that the salvation and cleansing that I will show you from the Bible is easy and straightforward. You need to pay close attention and read the actual verses in the Bible along with this text.

## POINT TWO

The key to understanding this salvation is to remember that God has put up with you for your whole life. Read Romans 2:4-6. He's been good to you and has borne and suffered you to live in your sins for a long period of time. He's just waiting to show you the riches that He has for you. Up to the point of salvation, Paul equates this to our despising God's offer of grace, the forgiveness of our sins. He's been leading you and waiting for you to repent. If you don't choose His pathway to salvation, He will view you as having a hardened heart and will consider you to be unforgiven, allowing you to one day die in your sins. At that time, you will suffer eternal judgment and consequences in hell for your sins. Realize that this is grace, complete and unmerited favor on your part, that you can be forgiven. All you need to see is that He is leading you to repent. Prepare to do so.

## POINT THREE

Realize that you have sinned and cannot match the sinless perfection that He requires to allow you to enter heaven (Romans 3:23). It matters little if the worst thing you've done is to tell a white lie, steal a pencil, or take the name of God in vain once as you cursed. Or, maybe you've committed murder, rape, and grand larceny and are a "big-time sinner." Just realize that breaking any of the Ten Commandments will land you in hell if you have not requested His forgiveness by the time you die. It may be that you've broken all of the Ten Commandments. In His eyes, if you are an unsaved person, you are a filthy and unclean spiritual leper who cannot be in His heaven. The only way God can accept you is if you accept His free gift of grace and be justified by the work that Jesus Christ has done to redeem you (Romans 3:24-25). For now, understand that being "justified" is a judicial or legal ruling by God that He has placed your sins on the work that Jesus did at the cross on Calvary and that you are forgiven. This ruling means that He views you as never having sinned in the past, present, or in the future. This will become clearer as we continue.

## POINT FOUR

Remember that God does love you. Romans 4:8-9 states that God gave us His love even when we were sinners. He sent Christ to die for us and allows us this method of justification by the blood He shed on Calvary. We have been saved from the wrath to come if we so choose to be. We have done nothing to earn it but be the lepers that we are. This is a true gift from Him that we do not deserve. He loves us, though we have never really shown love to Him.

Let me say this in another way. By Jesus Christ's death on the cross, He has already forgiven mankind and provided them a method to get to heaven. There is nothing left for you to do but accept this free offer. It is not automatic. You must personally accept His free offer in order to receive the grace of forgiveness.

## POINT FIVE

It becomes clear by this time that the eternal life that our sins have earned us is eternal death in hell (Romans 6:23). The gift of God, the alternative, is eternal life with God in heaven through Jesus Christ, our propitiation or offering made for our sins (Romans 3:25). Nothing we can do in life earns salvation for us, unless it is our acceptance of Jesus Christ's work on the cross. Think about your past sins. Commit to Him that you are not going to live in those sins any longer. You are now going to live for Him and dwell in His house. That's where He wants you. As we've already discussed in chapter 5 of this book, your life will now change when you pray for forgiveness and receive the free gift of salvation in faith. You'll no longer reside in a life of sin, but will reside with Him and He with you as He sends you His Holy

Spirit to live within you (Romans 8:9, 1 Corinthians 3:16). Repent, turn from your sins in prayer, and He will bring you out of them as He walks with you throughout your new life.

## POINT SIX

So, you ask, "If we can't earn it on our own, how do we get God's forgiveness and the hope of a future with Him?" "Faith in Jesus Christ" is the answer here. If you have allowed the Scriptures that you've read so far to penetrate and get down into your heart, you're beginning to have a little faith. That little bit of faith is all it takes to move toward attaining your salvation with Christ (Romans 10:8). Faith starts small. You've already begun to grow if you've realized that hearing the Word of God generates faith in the believer: "So then faith cometh by hearing, and hearing by the Word of God" (Romans 10:17). The Word has gotten close to you and is now in your heart and mouth as you have spoken it and taken these truths into your heart. So, if you confess your faith in Jesus to others and have believed in your heart that Jesus was raised from the dead by God, you are saved and are now going to live eternally with Him when the Lord takes you to your new heavenly home (Romans 10:9).

Romans 10:10 states that when man's heart, the deepest part of one's spiritual being, believes, it is given over to His righteousness. You need to make that decision now. Then, as verse ten continues, confessing it with your mouth is the point where you must not be ashamed to share your testimony and the gospel with others. If you do share it, He won't be ashamed to acknowledge you in return (Romans10:11).

You cannot attain salvation on your own. If you try to earn it on your own merit, you'll end up spending eternity in hell paying for your own sins. The only way to succeed is to place those sins on Jesus and His work at the cross. It is your choice to accept this free gift from Him.

Now is the time to think back on the ten lepers in Luke, chapter 17. The one Samaritan leper who returned gave Jesus sincere thanks and adoration (vs. 16). Realize now that you are just like that leper. You owe Christ everything. You have just received your life back from bondage, not only for this lifetime, but for eternity. You are now acceptable in His eyes and His Father's. The Holy Spirit resides within you and now guides your life through your study of the Word and your new conscience. This is now part of your testimony for Him, to His work within you, and it is to be shared with those around you. He has removed a fatal disease that would have continued to cripple you, causing you, your family, and your friends great pain. You should now be one of the most thankful people in the world. You owe this healing to Him. No one else but Jesus Christ could have healed you. Everything you will do will speak of your thankfulness for His work performed in you. This salvation that you now have makes you His. You are to thank and to serve Him. Be thankful and show it each and every day.

Really, there should have been ten ex-lepers joyfully leaping back to the Lord in a spirit of thanksgiving, rather than just one leaping ex-leper returning in thanks to Christ. When one thinks about it, this is typical of society both then and now. The average human being does not return thanks to the Lord nearly as much as he should. Rather, too many people take healing in stride as if it is their "just due" in life. It's not. The Lord may be blessing us and those around us even when He stops our progress through some illness and does not heal us. It is our duty to be open to the work that He may be doing through us when He doesn't do those things we had hoped that He would do. He knows what He is accomplishing, while at this present time, we do not.

We should remember to give thanks not only for the largest blessings but also for the smallest blessings: a smile, a glass of water, a pair of reading glasses, a ride to church, and so on. This list could obviously go on for pages and pages. Don't forget to give the Lord thanks for the smallest bodily function, the smallest morsel of food, or even the plainest piece of clothing you own.

We are told that we are even to give thanks in adversity and trials—they produce the blessings of the fruit of righteousness and the Lord's glory within us (2 Corinthians 4:17, Hebrews 12:11). It's not easy, but this is shown in the truth of God's Word. When we look back on some of our life's worst trials and see the great blessings that came out of them, we should give thanks and grow in faith. We are to give thanks in everything (1 Thessalonians 5:18).

As a matter of personal testimony, I can assure you that the Lord has a way to make things work out for good to those who love Him (Romans 8:28). The year was 1974. The first oil embargo was underway, and gasoline and fuels of all kinds were hard to obtain for vehicles throughout the United States and the world. Double-digit inflation was increasing the costs of food, fuel, and most of the items that Americans had considered "basic" in life, things such as rent, clothing, utilities, groceries, and hardware of all kinds.

My father owned a small grocery store and restaurant. Every load of groceries that he purchased to restock shelves during this period of time cost several percent more than the stock he was replacing. With already-low margins on the sale of groceries, he was spending more to restock the shelves than the store brought in as profit. Paying down debt for the store, paying for the cost of replacement stock, and simply paying operational costs such as power, water, and repairs was driving his little business under. Literally, he was in despair. He had asked family and friends only three years before to assist him in getting into his new business. They had graciously helped him with purchasing the business. In his mind, how could he go back to them and ask for more monetary support when it seemed as though the business would not be able to sustain itself any longer?

What made the situation seem worse is that he had been terminated from a long-term job with a local grocery distributor just four years earlier. He had been using alcohol heavily. When a former employee whom my father had fired just months earlier spotted my father consuming alcohol in his company-supplied car, the former-employee-turned-enemy reported the occurrence to the company. When my father was directed to come to the company president's office and was confronted with the report, my father admitted the truth. As the president told my father, he regrettably was forced to terminate my father immediately.

Talking with my father some time later as I worked for him part-time while attending technical school, he was quite circumspect and mature regarding the occurrence. He had made a mistake. Regardless of the circumstances that led to his own termination, he told me that he had broken the rules. He deserved, he'd stated, what he received. I remember being proud of him and how he had faced his own sin, though I didn't at that time know how to help him place the situation in the past. His actions had placed severe pressure on his marriage, our family's finances, and our future. From the outside looking in, I could see that he believed himself to be a failure. But, he did not stop his use and abuse of alcohol.

Personal history and its consequences, inability to pay his debtors, a marriage that was experiencing serious difficulties, an addiction to alcohol, and a lack of faith in the Lord Jesus Christ all converged and brought my father to the breaking point. Looking back, I can now see how depressed he was. After spending the night drinking heavily, he went out to his grocery store very early on the morning of December 11, 1974. When an employee arrived later that morning to open up for business hours, he found my father. He had committed suicide by hanging himself in the back of his grocery store.

This act of selfishness devastated my family. When I learned of it that morning, I was angry. How could a man that I believed to be so strong do that to himself? Not yet a Christian, I had no way to balance my views or come to a reasonable understanding of the deed. I was in shock, as was my wife and family.

I was twenty-one years of age, married, and had graduated from tech school the previous May. My wife and I had a daughter near the age of two and had moved away to start a career. Back home were my mother and my two youngest siblings, a sister and brother. My oldest two brothers have moved on to live their own lives a few years before. What were they to do now? My wife and I moved home to run the business until my mother was able to sell it, which occurred about six months later.

At this point, you are likely asking what this has to do with leprosy. A Catholic priest told me that my father was in hell and that there was nothing I could do about it. Offended, I told him that he might be right, but I asked him where he got the authority to make such a statement. He answered by saying that I was to accept "this fact" and forget about my father and not even pray for him. Neither did I like the answer nor did I believe it. I would find the answer to my question, whatever that answer might be. Again, Romans 8:28 comes into play here.

It took me five years of searching and questioning beliefs that I had been taught for a lifetime before I started down the correct path. While on business in Tacoma, Washington, I drove by a Christian book store. Thinking to myself that they may sell Bibles, and realizing that I did not have one, I stopped and purchased one. It had occurred to me that this book may have answers that I needed. I was about twenty-six years of age. Over the next two years, I read the Bible from cover to cover several times. Not only did that little Bible point out the answers to many of life's questions, including showing me a saving knowledge of Jesus Christ, but it stopped me in my tracks as I read Genesis 9:5.

Yes, I know that I should have picked up this answer from other verses that are far easier to understand, but this is the verse that answered the question for me. I had been "hung up" on a man having the power to say whether another man was condemned to hell. Genesis 9:5a states, "And surely your blood of your lives will I require." That jumped out at me. God is the judge, not mankind, of any man! This verse told me that we are going to be judged by Him for how we spend our lives, whether in waste or in productivity for Him. He would one day evaluate how we spent the time He gave us. God will know why a person committed suicide. Maybe that person was a godless heathen, and God "stated" that he needed to be condemned. Or, maybe that person was sick and needed to receive deeper evaluation by God.

Either way, I found comfort in the fact that God is in control. My father was an alcoholic. He had messed up in many areas of his life. However, I had learned one other important fact from my aunt—one of my father's sisters. She shared that my father had been saved, had trusted in Jesus Christ, when he was sixteen years old. Having by then read the Bible and given my own life to Christ through repentance and faith in the work that Jesus did for me on the cross, I saw that there is more to "this story." Was my father saved, or is he in hell as the priest stated? That, I now understand, is in God's hands.

I know this too. My father spent too long away from the Word as he allowed his family to be led and taught by a church that was not studying the Bible. As I look back, I can see where my father was still reading a tiny Army Bible that he had received while he served in the Army Air Corps in World War Two. Little things he would tell me when we were out working or traveling somewhere let me know that he was applying biblical principles where he could in life. Yes, he was a leper, ensconced in alcohol. But, now, understanding biblical principles and standards more clearly, I am able to state that my father failed in many things and succeeded in others. I have hope that his leprosy was cleansed, even though he didn't travel on to the maturity that he was supposed to have attained. I have hope that I'll see him in heaven. He may have allowed himself to be side-tracked and taken off the correct path, but where that path diverged is in God's hands and judgment.

As a result of this strange and sad turn of events, my father's suicide, I questioned my own salvation. That questioning led to my own salvation and that of my wife and children. Ultimately, God pointed to ministries that I would need to be involved with in order to win souls and disciple young Christians to greater maturity. These young Christians would lead others to Christ and maturity. This is the Lord's work, not mine. He receives the glory. And, maybe, I will get to see my father again in heaven. The Lord is in control, and I am happy for it. At this time, I know that mankind does not have the ability to judge another soul rightly.

Before we leave the specific topic of salvation, there are some things that will help you now as you leave your previous life of leprosy. First of all, you are now permanently cured of your leprosy. God makes us a promise when He tells us that this gift of salvation and His calling of us to Him are without repentance (Romans 11:29). In other words, your sincere prayer for the repentance of your sins and belief in His work on the cross allows God to see you through Jesus Christ's work on the cross. He's placed your sins on the work that Christ did as the only sinless man to have ever died, falsely accused and murdered on a cross. In God's eyes, you are now cleansed and spotless. Don't forget that this is not through your own works. By placing your faith in Jesus Christ, you are saved by His grace so that you and I can't boast on this salvation. It's His work, not ours (Ephesians 2:8-9).

Next, keep in mind is that you are immediately cleansed (1 John 1:7). If we now have fellowship with Christ, if we now have salvation, then He has cleansed us and we are walking in the light. We read that He has done the washing away of our sins with His own blood and that He will be the faithful witness for us (Revelation 1:5). We are washed and cleansed and do not need to carry our old sins with us.

Let's call this "immediate sanctification" or cleansing. Again, none of our sins will be held against us by God when we stand before Him since Jesus Christ will testify for us because of our profession of faith and our reliance on His work on the cross. We are now ex-lepers who are spotless before Christ. We can now start the process of rejoining society, ending our forced isolation from it.

Where does the work start for the ex-leper during this new walk with Christ? Because we are now cleansed, we want to live a life of purity for Him. This is where the ex-leper is going to need to take it slow in order to stay pure, making changes that allow our lives to conform to this new Christian walk. We, as ex-lepers, have a lot of old "bad habits" that need to be broken, and there are new "good habits" that must be formed. Let's call this "progressive sanctification."

Yes, we are already cleansed and sanctified as holy in God's eyes, but now the work to stay holy and progress in the maturity Jesus wants for us must start. No, a person will not lose his salvation if he sins here or there. We will now, though, hate sin, whereas before we may have loved and coddled our preferred sins. When we "fall" into the occasional temptation and sin, we will find no pleasure in the sin, experiencing guilt and loss of His fellowship while we're out of touch with God during our fall. So, the work to stay pure starts, moment by moment and day by day.

The cleansed leper now has promises to cling to in his or her new life with Christ (2 Corinthians 7:1). Life is brighter because, regardless of what happens now, whether death occurs in the short or the long term, the ex-leper knows the outcome. He has eternity with Christ as a promise within his breast. The cleaning starts now in the area around the leper. The "filthiness of the flesh and spirit" must be purged from one's life.

The taverns and bars are now off-limits since the leper cannot trust himself with alcohol. The magazines, movies, and Internet sites must all be thrown out since the lust of the eyes can be a significant problem for the ex-leper. Not only that, but if the cured leper must use a computer with Internet access, the screen should be visible to all who pass by, whether it be the wife, children, or coworkers. Doors to the computer room will now remain open at all times. The street corner where one used to purchase drugs is now forbidden, and there will be no "second trip of temptation" around that block. The casinos and gambling houses are now prohibited. A trusted individual will handle the ex-leper's money and credit cards for a long time to come. The tongue, gossip, cursing, blasphemy, and aspects regarding the use of one's voice must also be tamed, and it may take some people a lifetime to do so. Many of these limitations may be in place for the life of the ex-leper. It may be that the Lord removes all of the temptations of these "favorite sins" from the cured person, but, while this healing is still fresh, it is best to allow no chance for relapses to the illness.

The use of an accountability partner must now be a high consideration. Someone who is strong and not tempted with the particular "favorite ex-sin of the ex-leper" will be a certain need for a prolonged period of time. The partner should be of the same sex. It is rarely successful for the spouse to be an accountability partner. As this isn't specifically a book on counseling of addictions, we won't cover much more depth here.

Last of all in the verse, the goal for the recovering leper is to grow in holiness. The idea of a goal for the ex-leper is apt. Why should the leper care so much that he or she be purged from all sin and perversion? This ex-leper is a wealth of knowledge about the sins to which he was addicted. Once out of their own addictions, they can spot the lies that are being told by others and can also suggest excellent ways to get out and stay out of the particular addiction. God desires that this person work to reach other people (2 Timothy 2:21-26) and, therefore, the ex-leper must have his life completely scrubbed of any material that could cause a recurring problem for him. By staying clean, this person can now go forth and help others out of the things he was addicted to, being careful not to allow himself to be pulled back into sin (Galatians 6:1, 2 Corinthians 1:3-4). People who are in addiction listen quite readily to those who WERE in their addiction. They have a common bond, and the present addict can then see from the past addict that there is a way out of sin. A cleansed ex-leper can be a great morale booster to those lepers who are in need of cleansing.

This life of "progressive sanctification" creates a great healing of the heart. As new Christians draw closer to God, they may not forget all of the things that they did or how they did them, but these areas of their history dim as time elapses (James 4:8). The damage to their hearts is now healing. They don't feel as compelled to get back into addiction, and they are drawn closer to wanting to do God's work and perform the walk He has for them. This "double-mindedness," where they still picture themselves as a leper—an alcoholic, a sex-addict, a gambler, a drug addict, a liar, a thief, and so on—who is trying to get away from the old bad habits in order to start new ones that are worthwhile in the eyes of God, is diminishing. They are moving from this double-mindedness of being a "leper and ex-leper" to the single-mindedness of being an ex-leper striving to become closer to God and His work. No longer do they try to fake out the people who are around them but are becoming truthful and holy in all they attempt to do in life.

As a spiritual leper (the unsaved person), one has no hope. Life for the leper is purposeless, fruitless, and ends in a dark death in the grave. The leper's existence is a life that is presently hopeless and ends in a death that is eternally hopeless. This hopelessness makes a person desperate. The leper sees his life moving toward being totally crippled and helpless. Though their bodies are misshapen, their faces disfigured, and their limbs non-functional in any original sense, they are desperate to find a cure for their illness of addiction to sin in order to extend their lives here on earth. Living this life of desperate hopelessness, the leper no longer has a reason to live a good clean life. They may as well, in their view, continue their downward spiral into the filth and squalor their bodies are now lying upon since they cannot be mobile on their own. We now know that this is not necessary. They simply do not have the right method in which to be cured. We need to guide them to the cure.

We now know that we can offer the leper hope. Though the leper may have the consequences of sin that include a sentence in jail, the loss of a spouse who "couldn't take it any longer," an alienated family, health lost due to alcohol, food, and drug addictions, and the Lord's blessings of earthly wealth lost because of the leper's own poor stewardship during an addiction, the Christian ex-leper has hope. This is the time to rebuild one's physical health and reestablish relationships with family and friends. It is the time to talk openly in order to reopen doors that had closed when the leper had alienated the people around him. With the leprosy having been cured and the leper having been "released from the prison of sin," the healing of previously-destroyed relationships can now start.

With hope, the cleansed leper has this continual duty to purify himself (1 John 3:3). The simple idea that we are now God's property should give us the joy and gratitude with which we strive to be more like Him every day. We don't fully succeed in being completely like Him in this life, but one day when we are face to face with Him, we will be like Him (1 John 3:2). One day, when we are with Him, we will no longer be able to sin (Romans 6:7). There will be full fellowship with Him, and we will not have the ability to separate ourselves from Him with sin at any time in eternity. This will truly be glorious, and the glory will be given to Him. This is our hope for eternity!

Think about what has happened. As a leper, the sin we wallowed in was destroying us. We had neither a good future nor any hope. This is all changed when we come to a saving knowledge of Him.  Look at the comparisons between the spiritual leper and the forgiven Christian:

# BEFORE
## WITH LEPROSY

We are born infected with sin. We will die of it.

---

We are encumbered by sin's effects on our lives.

---

Sin is hidden for a while.

---

As sin progresses in our lives, it becomes more visible to others.

---

Our lives become covered with lies and deception.

---

As we go deeper into sin, we are isolated from those we love.

---

In sin, we stood afar off from society as we were grouped with other sinners.

---

In deep sin, life starts to completely fall apart.

---

Death and hell are the result of lives lived in sin.

---

The sinner has nothing but judgment and hell for eternity.

# **AFTER**
# CLEANSED

We are cured by His forgiveness when we have faith in Jesus' work on the cross.

---

Saved, we now have sensitivity to God and the things of God.

---

Sin is forgotten by God.

---

Sins are erased by God. Sin lessens as the Christian matures in Christ Jesus.

---

As forgiven Christian, we now live a life that is lived openly for God.

---

When we are forgiven, we are brought into God's family for eternity.

---

Now, as Christians, we are grouped with other believers.

---

As forgiven Christians, purpose for our lives is restored.

---

Judgment occurred at the cross, and no future judgment of sin occurs for the Christian.

---

The Christian looks forward to eternal life with God and is eternally at home in heaven.

As seen in the table above, there is the difference of night and day when comparing the life with and without leprosy. The fear and despair that we had in life have disappeared. Once we have grasped the fact that God has forgiven us before we even sin, we are free to change our lives and move forward as we allow the Holy Spirit to change our desires and lifestyle. Though we have "fits and starts" in our walk, we are living a walk that is progressively growing closer and closer to Him. He knows that we are not yet perfect and gives us the tools in His gifts (Galatians 5:22-23) and strength to continue on through the trial He has allowed into our lives to mature us.

We look ahead to places that we now may be able to serve Him, doing more for Him as our own maturity advances. Now, our lives are given in self-chosen self-sacrifice to Him as we fully realize that this is our joyous duty in life. Romans 12:1 states that we now present our bodies as living sacrifices, holy and acceptable to Him, and that this is logical or reasonable service to Him. And, there is so much for us to do! We are able to teach, live lives in Christian ministry to others, live lives of leadership for Christ, love our brothers and sisters in Christ, serve one another, doing so in trials and tribulations, giving to the saints in the name of Jesus Christ, acting as a shoulder to cry on, and a fan to cheer our fellow Christians onward, while avoiding a life of evil and hypocrisy (Romans 12:7-15).

The leper has become an overcomer. The life of sin has straightway moved from sin to salvation to a life of faith and service. Because the leper has made this choice, he or she inherits all of the good things promised by God to the believer (Revelation 21:7). Salvation, heaven, strength and confidence in one's daily walk, and "Sonship" of Jesus Christ are only a short list of items supplied to the believer upon this adoption to Jesus' family, the church. All of the promises of God are now owned by the believer.

A caution is due the person who has not made this choice of salvation by faith alone in the work of Jesus Christ. If you've still held your place in Revelation 21:7, read the very next verse. If you are not open to this verse, I strongly suggest that you open your Bible to Revelation 21:8. It gives the reader a condensed list of "personal soul conditions" that will keep the person out of heaven, sending him to hell and, consequently, to the lake of fire and brimstone for eternity.

The first item listed is "fear." Christ rebukes doubt or fear and calls it lack of faith in Mark 4:40. In John 14:27, Jesus has addressed the actions that Judas Iscariot has brought to pass and states that He will love those who follow His Word. He will live with those who follow Him (John 14:23-26). But, if a person does not do so, the person is not of God. On the flip side, the believer receives the Comforter, the Holy Spirit, who teaches the believer all things. He assures the believer in verse 27 not to be afraid. We should have peace in our hearts, not fear, as new believers in Christ. We are given the power of love and a sound mind in Jesus Christ, not the spirit of fear (2 Tim. 1:7-8). In 2 Timothy 1:8, it equates fear with those who are ashamed to share the gospel as their own personal testimony, as opposed to the example of Paul, who is not fearful of giving his own testimony of affliction for the work of Jesus Christ. Don't worry, when times are at their worst, Jesus will place His words in our mouths in order to provide a testimony for Him (Luke 21:15). Do not let a spirit of fear come between you and salvation.

The second item listed in Revelation 21:8 is "unbelieving." Belief, in and of itself, is expected by Jesus Christ of all people in the world. Those who do not want to believe in the work that Christ has done for them on the cross are allowed to believe in themselves or the work of others as they pay for their own sins during an eternity in the lake of fire. Simply put, not believing in Christ is a choice that comes with eternal consequences.

The remainder of the list of items that will send an unbeliever to hell for eternity is significantly the same as the longer list studied in Galatians 5:19-21. Yes, this list is shorter, but it includes all those who are held within their sins: the abominable (bdelusso), which are those disgusting people who stink of sins of all kinds. It includes those who are caught up in the murder of their fellow man, as well as whoremongers (pornos)—those who are caught up in prostitution, sexual debauchery, fornication, and whoring. Again, it lists sorcerers, who are the same as those who are into the drugs and witchcraft we discussed in chapter 5 of this book. Idolaters are listed again. As you remember, this is anyone who places any of the things in life before his or her commitment to God.

It is interesting to note that "liars" (pseudes: untrue, erroneous, deceitful, wicked, false) are listed within their own category in Revelation 21:8. Why is that? The Book of Revelation is also called the Book of the Apocalypse as given to John, the Apostle. It is a book of the end times. As an account of how God will bring all earthly things to an end, this book relates the lies that mankind has promulgated or endorsed throughout history. During this time period specifically focused upon within the Book of Revelation, the seven years of the Tribulation and then the 1,000-year Millennial Reign of Jesus Christ upon earth, man is judged for his lies and abominations upon the earth with the intent of waking him up and bringing him to a saving knowledge of Jesus Christ. The world—everyone—is admonished to heed Christ's words in this book and to hear Him as He requests this change of heart to come to Him and receive His offer of salvation (Revelation 3:15-22, 22:7, 12, 17).

After going through a long list of character traits of end-times man in 2 Timothy 3:1-7, Paul tells Timothy that the time will come when man lives in his lies (2 Timothy 4:3-4). These evil times occur when man personally chooses not to listen to sound doctrine—the truths taught in God's Word (2 Timothy 4:3). They go after their own lusts, their personal desires, and knowingly allow other men to teach to their itching ears (vs. 3). These are "ears" that don't want to hear what God dictates for their lives. Instead, they are turning to the lies of men by turning from the truth to fables (vs. 4). Fables are understood to be tales and fictions. This is where man believes silly mysteries that are unproven and unsanctioned by God in His Word. Whether one likes to hear it or not, these teachings include fables such as false religions, evolution, witchcraft, ungodly gain or wealth, sexual license, abortion, and following governments who have left the principles of God's Word. This list, today, would grow to be quite sizable if we continued on with it. It definitely looks as though man is living in the end times.

It is time to get serious about your faith and to avoid these lies at all costs. We must know the Word in order to know the lies and avoid being misled. If you are still unconvinced that you need the Lord Jesus Christ as your Savior, read again from chapter 5 forward within this book and evaluate yourself and your life. You will not gain entry into heaven without Christ. The times are soon coming to an end, and Jesus is on the way back in judgment (Revelation 22:7, 20). He will not come as a lamb when He comes to earth for the second time, but rather as the Conqueror and King (Revelation 19:11-16). If you are not a believer, it will not go well for you. It is my prayer that you receive the Lord Jesus Christ as your Savior at this moment.

# 8: CLEANSED REFLECTIONS

As we look back on what we've studied, it's time to ask ourselves, "Are we making a difference?" Are we allowing ourselves to be used by God to do His work? It is our duty to take our personal feelings out of the personal evaluation we are making of ourselves in order to look objectively and impartially at ourselves as Christians. We need to understand what we've done for those around us who are currently leprous. It is our job to evaluate what we've done for those who have accepted Christ Jesus as their Savior. These are the people who now need discipling or teaching in order for them to mature and have the ability to carry the salvation message of the gospel to the people who are within their circles of acquaintance. We need to be about the Lord's work as He outlined it in the Great Commission in Matthew 28:19 and 20: to teach (the winning of souls), baptize, and disciple (the maturing of new believers). Another way of saying this is as follows:

1 We are first called to conversion in Jesus Christ. We are personally saved.

2 We are to call or win souls to Christ (Matthew 28:19).

**3** We are to baptize and bring people into the local church (Matthew 28:19).

**4** We are directed to commission those new church members to be mature and work in the church too (Matthew 28:20).

We were once lepers. It is now our duty to help other lepers be cured. They too must be taught the saving knowledge of Jesus Christ and then must rearrange their lives to serve Christ.

Reflect on how the world has been affected by the life of Jesus Christ since He walked the earth some two thousand years ago. He is the only God-made-man to have ever walked the earth, and He turned the world upside down. He did so in a way that has been good for the world. His effect on the world remains today and will remain until the world is "shut down" after His millennial reign on earth.

We can all name people who turned the world upside down to do evil. People like most Caesars, Hitler, Mussolini, Stalin, and Saddam Hussein are likely the names on the tips of our tongues. Though they left destruction and death in their collective wakes, those effects were temporary. Not to minimize the devastation they caused, but their work was turned around or corrected by others almost as soon as they were off the scene of their own brutal regime. These people simply gave greater mankind a rallying point with a sign that says, "Don't be like this person!" These people were true lepers, stinking and crippled in their sins.

It must also be stated that there are those who tried to make the world a better place. We've already mentioned Hansen and his work on the disease of leprosy, our topic. D. L. Moody has already been mentioned in this book because of his heart for and work in evangelism. One could list Dr. Jonas Salk for his development of the polio vaccine in 1955.[57] Martin Luther could be listed for his personal effort to bring the world back to true Christianity. World leaders galore could be listed for trying to make the world a better place. But, none of these people turned the world upside down as did Jesus Christ.

Jesus Christ showed the power of His Godhood through His miracles, His example, His preaching, and His work with both the sinner and the saved. He provided the path of salvation for all of mankind through the allowance of His own personal death, a death that was illegal, unfounded, and vicious. He truly was a lamb led to slaughter. No man has ever shown mankind the love that He showed to us. Reflect on His love for us.

Ponder the fact that Christ normally worked with people one on one. Why then did He work with the ten lepers? Having personally taught and preached to many groups that are known to contain unsaved attendees, I know that "group mentality" is a normal occurrence. One can observe the general audience as one teaches or preaches. People are changed for a moment, and they see the need for change within themselves. Their need and pain are visible upon their faces. They feel the tug of the Holy Spirit as they are convicted of sin or, even more extensively, of a lifestyle that is morally depraved and degenerate. This effect of the gospel is apparent on many people. But, neither I nor mankind is capable of reading the heart of another human being (1 Samuel 16:7, John 2:25) for sure. The Holy Spirit does the tugging to get them out of their seats to walk forward for salvation.

As the altar call ends, though, they have already left the service or are now less convicted since the message has ended and they are no longer under the watchful eye of God and the preacher. They're able to blend into the group and can escape the pressure placed upon them by the Lord. It may be that a fellow attendee has given them "permission" to check out without going forward because they're "a good person." However, no one is good enough. This point has been made clear in this book. Everyone begins as a leper. Everyone is stained by sin, and no one can make it to heaven on his or her own. But, for whatever the reason, the "group" is harder to reach than the individual.

The "ratio" of salvation from a group is lower than that where the gospel is presented to the individual. In the case of the ten lepers, one person was thankful enough to come back and thank and worship Christ. Nine were surely happy to have been affected by Christ but did not leave the crowd to come back to Christ in order to verify their own cleansing and salvation through Christ Himself. That's a ninety percent failure ratio. And these men had truly and personally been changed by Christ. They hadn't simply heard a preaching message but had received personal healing from a devastating illness.

Reflect on your need to show Christ true gratitude and worship for what He has done, is doing, and will do in your life. One day, you will be in heaven with Him if you are a Christian. Will you be embarrassed by your own lackadaisical attitude toward Him when He deserved enthusiasm toward His work in you?

Think about the fact that the Samaritan came back to give personal thanks and worship to Christ Jesus. Evidently, this man alone was a Samaritan, the half-breed (half Syrian and half Jew). The others must have been full-blooded Jews. The Samaritan was the down-trodden one of the ten. He would have been accepted only in Samaria and would have been considered an outsider, or racially impure, in any other region in Judea. When compared to the other nine, he was the outsider even though they were as sick as he was. Reflect on Jesus' methods. He didn't mind working with crowds or individuals. He didn't care what they looked like. Whether to those who are "accepted," or those who are not, we can minister to all.

They were all poor. They were all outcasts. They were all sick and wasted in their leprosy. Yet, the tenth leper came back. Jesus states that it is easier for a camel to go through the eye of a needle than for a rich man to enter into the kingdom of God (Matthew 19:24). But,

Christ didn't say that it was impossible, as all things are possible with God (Matthew 19:26). The downtrodden aren't the only ones who need salvation, and they aren't the only ones who can be saved. The rich can be saved, but too many times they are too sure of their own wealth and ability to save themselves. God counsels the rich in Revelation 3:17 and 18 to realize that they are pitiable, poor, and naked in His eyes and that all they need to do is accept His gold, His salvation, and allow Him to anoint them to be with Him. The rich are wasted lepers just like the poor, though they do not often choose Christ for their healing.

There are many levels and kinds of worldly wealth, though here we'll talk about areas of business that have obtained their wealth under less than honorable circumstances. Today, we can see the wealthy whose money is made by obtaining the earth's riches of oil, minerals, precious metals, and the like—not necessarily bad, unless the methodology used is one of "ravaging" the earth. We can see the people who traffic in human misery, such as prostitution, drugs, alcohol, the sale of the young, all for the pleasure of their clients. We see the wealthy who usurp the labor of the world in order to grow their own personal bank accounts.

The work that many of the rich perform is venerable, like that of the doctor, the average business man, the manufacturer, or the trader. Some of the work done by the wealthy is good, and God is trying to refine the wealthy, just as gold is refined in the fire. If only the wealthy would allow themselves to be refined, they would see that their wealth is good and does not need to be hoarded. They can use the reasonable profits that they make to help those who are poor or who need the assistance the wealthy can provide to advance a godly need or cause. This isn't happening for the most part. When it occurs, it must be done in the Lord's name in order for it not to be burned as chaff in the fire (Matthew 3:12). Reflect on the fact that the wealthy are as downtrodden as the poor. They need salvation from their leprous conditions too.

Think about how the lepers stood afar off from Christ and called out to Him for cleansing. They wouldn't have known for sure that He would come through for them, but they seemed assured enough that they did not run to Him and "mob" him. They kept their cool.

We're the same way. We don't know how He will affect our lives, but we know He will change us just the same. He promised that He would come to us in so many ways (John 14:3, 18, 23, 4:19). He has chosen to heal us and affect our lives. He will do so, just as He did the ten lepers.

But, for even the most fervent believer in Christ, Jesus can seem afar off on occasion. For an example, we can look into the Old Testament where the priests were not doing their job. They weren't healing leprosy. God didn't seem to be close to the Hebrews of that time period, and the priests could have eased that distance by working with the people. Jesus must be brought to our fellow man by us. This is our work. Reflect on whether you are doing the proper work needed today in order to bring Christ closer to the lepers around you.

We have groups of leprous people walking around today. They're sick and dying and do not know it. They are impure in God's eyes and have no cure, at least as they presently understand their own plight. In David F. Wells' book, The Courage to Be Protestant,[58] Wells reinforces the idea that the Old Testament believer was not doing the job assigned to him by God. The people remained blind and deaf, and their hearts were hardened. In our terms for this book, the people were leprous.

Today, Wells reiterates, the church is also not doing its job, neither by sitting comfortably in its own salvation nor by doing enough to change the situation. We are neglecting our jobs. Comparatively, our churches are wealthy with nice buildings, wealthy members, and big budgets, but not enough is being done for the desperate in the third-world nations. Work to decrease the disparate nature of the world needs to be increased. No, this is not a call for the redistribution of wealth; this refers to the assistance needed to narrow that gap for those who are unable to help themselves. Let me clarify these statements. Are our churches helping those around the world? Did churches in the USA help those who suffered from damage in Hurricane Katrina? Yes, churches are helping. It is proper to refrain from blanket statements that might suggest that we're not doing anything to help those around us. I believe that Wells is suggesting that we do more. I believe that the Lord is asking us to do more.

Since it looks as though we are in the end times, should we focus less on the physical building or "house" of the church and more on the mission of the church? Reflect on how you can become more involved in the work of the missions within your church. Have you ignored the Lord's calling to become a missionary or to at least travel and work with missionaries for short periods of time as your work and schedule permit? Now is the time to be working ever harder at the work God has given us.

As of today, the nation of Israel has continually rejected Christ as the Messiah of the world. Superstition, ignorance, self-interest, and ingratitude are all signs that Israel has possessed throughout the centuries. Those outside the nation at least seemingly accept Him more readily. Unfortunately, the United States of America seems to be moving away from its alliance with Israel, having moved to support its own oil interests instead. With these statements having been made, it may help the reader to have a definition of a biblically sound role of support of Israel.

Turn to the book of Genesis to follow along with this call to support Israel. Abram (later to be called "Abraham") is told to move from his home land, that he will be the father of a great nation, and that he would be greatly blessed (Genesis 12:1-2). He is also told that God will bless those who bless his nation and curse those who curse his nation (Genesis 12:3). These statements in Genesis are pre-Mosaic Law and are thus still in effect. Since Abram is the father of the Israelite nation, we need to be careful to support Israel and not to curse it or "call it down." The Lord set aside an inheritance to the people of Israel and stated that the Lord's portion is His People (Deuteronomy 32:8-9). Not only that, the Lord found this people in the desert and instructed them, calling them the "apple of His eye" (Deuteronomy 32:10). If Israel is the apple of God's eye, and it is, we should be careful not to put God's eye out! In fact, God affirms that they are the apple of His eye when He states that He will shake His hand at any nation that touches Israel in the wrong way and He will spoil them (Zechariah 2:8-9).

One thing more needs to be included here. This directive given us to support Israel is not only an Old Testament instruction. As the Tribulation has comes to an end, Jesus will return as King of the Earth. In Matthew 25, He tells us that goat nations will need to be separated from sheep nations. Goat nations will go into everlasting punishment, and sheep nations will join with Him in the inheritance of the kingdom. Why is this so? Jesus' discourse in Matthew 24 and 25 is given in regards to Israel. Whoever has helped Him, His nation, with food, water, shelter, clothing, assistance with sickness, and by visiting them in prison, He will call righteous and they will join Him in the kingdom (Matthew 25:33-40). Those who have not helped will be sent to everlasting punishment (Matthew 25:41-46). All nations that gather against His nation Israel at the end of the Tribulation will be destroyed (Revelation 19:19-21). All those whom He accepts will be ushered into the Millennial Age to live under His Kingship (Revelation 20:4).

Though Israel may not always do things in biblical fashion, it is the role of all nations in the world to support her. Even if nations cannot convince her to do things biblically, it is the duty of these Gentile nations to work with her and guide her to work biblically as they are able. Even if Israel does not respond well, no nation on earth is to lift a hand against Israel.

Though this situation of not supporting Israel can be turned around to be more in line with the Bible, what can Christians do to help awaken our nation to resolve to return its support to Israel? Though Israel is a leprous nation at present, they will not be for long. Let's reflect on how we can assist in removing their spiritual leprosy. They are beginning to listen. Can we aid them in hearing?

I believe that it is fitting that we end this book with gratitude for the Lord Jesus. He is in control. People are being won to Christ because He is in control. We are being blessed because He watches over the believer and promises that the believer, the righteous person, will flourish and will be one day forever with Him. He is our Rock on which we can stand. In Christ, it will all turn out well in the end. If you are not with Christ, it will not turn out well for you.

Read Psalm 92 to grasp the feeling of gratitude that we need to have for all of the things the Lord has done for us. Praise Him! The believer is no longer leprous! Be fruitful and multiply.

## PSALM 92

¹ *It is a good thing to give thanks unto the Lord, and to sing praises unto thy name, O most High:*

² *To shew forth thy loving kindness in the morning, and thy faithfulness every night,*

³ *Upon an instrument of ten strings, and upon the psaltery; upon the harp with a solemn sound.*

⁴ *For thou, Lord, hast made me glad through thy work: I will*

*triumph in the works of thy hands.*

⁵ *O Lord, how great are thy works! And thy thoughts are very deep.*

⁶ *A brutish man knoweth not; neither doth a fool understand this.*

⁷ *When the wicked spring as the grass, and when all the workers of iniquity do flourish; it is that they shall be destroyed for ever:*

⁸ *But thou, Lord, art most high for evermore.*

⁹ *For, lo, thine enemies, O Lord, for, lo, thine enemies shall perish; all the workers of iniquity shall be scattered.*

¹⁰ *But my horn shalt thou exalt like the horn of the unicorn: I shall be anointed with fresh oil.*

¹¹ *Mine eyes also shall see my desire on mine enemies, and mine ears shall hear my desire of the wicked that rise up against me.*

¹² *The righteous shall flourish like the palm tree: he shall grow like a cedar in Lebanon.*

¹³ *Those that be planted in the house of the Lord shall flourish in the courts of our God.*

¹⁴ *They shall still bring forth fruit in old age; they shall be fat and flourishing;*

¹⁵ *To shew that the Lord is upright: he is my rock, and there is not unrighteousness in him.*

Amen!

# APPENDIX A:
## ENDNOTES

1    "Father_Damien," (http://www.aoc.gov/cc/art/nsh/damien. cfm). Capitol Campus/Art. The Architect of the Capitol. http:// www.aoc.gov/cc/art/nsh/damien.cfm. Retrieved 2012-03-26.

2    John Tayman, The Colony: The Harrowing True Story of the Exiles of Molokai (New York: Simon and Schuster, 2007)

3    Lew Wallace, Ben Hur, A Tale Of The Christ (1880)

4    www.Merckmanuals.com/home/print/infections/turberculosis_and_leprosy/leprosy.html  MMHE - Leprosy

5    www.Merckmanuals.com/home/print/infections/turberculosis_and_leprosy/leprosy.html  MMHE - Leprosy

6    www.stanford.edu/group/parasites/ParaSites2005/Leprosy/clinical.html – Symptoms

**7**     G Robbins, VM Tripathy, VN Misra, RK Mohanty, VS Shinde, et al. "Ancient Skeletal Evidence for Leprosy in India" (2000 B.C.) PLoS ONE 4(5): e5669. doi:10.1371/journal.pone.0005669 (2009).

**8**     www.stanford.edu/group/parasites/ParaSites2005/Leprosy/clinical.html – Modern History of Leprosy

**9**     Syphilis through history  (http://www.britannica.com/EBchecked/topic/578770/syphillis/253277/Syphilis-through-history#ref252973)  Encyclopædia Britannica

**10**    Unger's Bible Dictionary, (Nineteenth Printing 1973), Leprosy, 266.

**11**    Bauer, Danker, Arndt, and Gingrich, A Greek-English Lexicon of the New Testament and other Christian Literature, (The University of Chicago Press, 2000), Lepra, 592.

**12**    Kingdom of Heaven, 20th Century Fox, Produced and Directed by Ridley Scott, 2005.

**13**    James Strong, Strong's Exhaustive Concordance of the Bible, (Thomas Nelson Publishers, 1990), Tsara, Strong's #6879

**14**    Brown-Driver-Briggs Hebrew and English Lexicon (2nd Printing, Dec 1996), 863-864.

**15**    James Strong, Strong's Exhaustive Concordance of the Bible (Thomas Nelson Publishers, 1990), Tsaraath, Strong's #6883

**16**    Brown-Driver-Briggs Hebrew and English Lexicon (2nd Printing, Dec 1996), 863.

**17**    Bauer, Danker, Arndt, and Gingrich, A Greek-English Lexicon of the New Testament and other Christian Literature (The University of Chicago Press, 2000), Lepis compared with Leprao, 592.

**18**    Bauer, Danker, Arndt, and Gingrich, A Greek-English Lexicon of the New Testament and other Christian Literature (The University of Chicago Press, 2000), Lepra or Lepras or Lepre, 592.

**19**    Bauer, Danker, Arndt, and Gingrich, A Greek-English Lexicon of the New Testament and other Christian Literature (The University of Chicago Press, 2000), Lepros or Lepra or Lepron or Leproi, 592.

**20**    D. A. Carson, Douglas J. Moo, and Leon Morris, An Introduction to the New Testament (Grand Rapids: Zondervan, 2005), 204-205.

**21**    Everett Ferguson, Backgrounds of Early Christianity (3rd Edition, Eerdmans Publishing, 2003), 562.

**22**    Merrill F. Unger, Unger's Bible Dictionary (Moody Press, 1973), Samaritan, 958-960.

**23**    Charles Caldwell Ryrie, Ryrie KJV Study Bible, (Moody Publishers, 1994), 1549.

**24**    Merrill F. Unger, Unger's Bible Dictionary (Moody Press, 1973), Samaritan, 960.

**25** Leon Morris, The Gospel According to Matthew (Intervarsity Press, 1992), geenna, 115.

**26** Strong's #2919: krino: to try, condemn, or punish

**27** Strong's #350: anakrino; to scrutinize, examine, and discern

**28** Bauer, Danker, Arndt, and Gingrich, A Greek-English Lexicon of the New Testament and other Christian Literature (The University of Chicago Press, 2000), page 656, moicheia

**29** Bauer, Danker, Arndt, and Gingrich, A Greek-English Lexicon of the New Testament and other Christian Literature (The University of Chicago Press, 2000), page 854, porneia

**30** Bauer, Danker, Arndt, and Gingrich, A Greek-English Lexicon of the New Testament and other Christian Literature (The University of Chicago Press, 2000), page 34, akatharsia

**31** Bauer, Danker, Arndt, and Gingrich, A Greek-English Lexicon of the New Testament and other Christian Literature (The University of Chicago Press, 2000), page 141, aselgeia

**32** Bauer, Danker, Arndt, and Gingrich, A Greek-English Lexicon of the New Testament and other Christian Literature (The University of Chicago Press, 2000), page 280, eidololatreia

**33** Bauer, Danker, Arndt, and Gingrich, A Greek-English Lexicon of the New Testament and other Christian Literature (The University of Chicago Press, 2000), page 1049, pharmakeia

**34** Edward T. Welch, Blame it on the Brain? (P & R Publishing, 1998), pages 105-106; Robert D. Smith M.D., The Christian Counselor's Medical Desk Reference (2000), pages 63-70.

**35** Bauer, Danker, Arndt, and Gingrich, A Greek-English Lexicon of the New Testament and other Christian Literature (The University of Chicago Press, 2000), echthra, 419.

**36** Bauer, Danker, Arndt, and Gingrich, A Greek-English Lexicon of the New Testament and other Christian Literature (The University of Chicago Press, 2000), eris, 392.

**37** Bauer, Danker, Arndt, and Gingrich, A Greek-English Lexicon of the New Testament and other Christian Literature (The University of Chicago Press, 2000), zelos, 427.

**38** Bauer, Danker, Arndt, and Gingrich, A Greek-English Lexicon of the New Testament and other Christian Literature (The University of Chicago Press, 2000), thumos, 461-462.

**39** Bauer, Danker, Arndt, and Gingrich, A Greek-English Lexicon of the New Testament and other Christian Literature (The University of Chicago Press, 2000), eritheia, page 392.

**40** Bauer, Danker, Arndt, and Gingrich, A Greek-English Lexicon of the New Testament and other Christian Literature (The University of Chicago Press, 2000), dichostasia, 252-253.

41   Bauer, Danker, Arndt, and Gingrich, A Greek-English Lexicon of the New Testament and other Christian Literature (The University of Chicago Press, 2000), hairesis, 27-28.

42   Bauer, Danker, Arndt, and Gingrich, A Greek-English Lexicon of the New Testament and other Christian Literature (The University of Chicago Press, 2000), phthonos, 1054.

43   Bauer, Danker, Arndt, and Gingrich, A Greek-English Lexicon of the New Testament and other Christian Literature (The University of Chicago Press, 2000), phonos, 1063.

44   Bauer, Danker, Arndt, and Gingrich, A Greek-English Lexicon of the New Testament and other Christian Literature (The University of Chicago Press, 2000), methe, 625.

45   Bauer, Danker, Arndt, and Gingrich, A Greek-English Lexicon of the New Testament and other Christian Literature (The University of Chicago Press, 2000), komos, 580.

46   Bauer, Danker, Arndt, and Gingrich, A Greek-English Lexicon of the New Testament and other Christian Literature (The University of Chicago Press, 2000), toigaroun, 1009.

47   Bauer, Danker, Arndt, and Gingrich, A Greek-English Lexicon of the New Testament and other Christian Literature (The University of Chicago Press, 2000), homoiosis, 708.

48   Bauer, Danker, Arndt, and Gingrich, A Greek-English Lexicon of the New Testament and other Christian Literature (The University of Chicago Press, 2000), poieo, 839, 840, 3c.

**49** Bauer, Danker, Arndt, and Gingrich, A Greek-English Lexicon of the New Testament and other Christian Literature (The University of Chicago Press, 2000). meno, 630, 631, 1aB and 2a.

**50** Matthew Henry's Commentary on the Whole Bible, edited by Hendrickson (Hendrickson Publishers, 2005), Gal. 5:19-21 Comments, 2303.

**51** Walvoord and Zuck, The Bible Knowledge Commentary (Victor Books, 1986), 113.

**52** Charles Caldwell Ryrie, The Ryrie Study Bible (Moody Publishers, 1994), 233, and King James Bible Commentary, by Thomas Nelson Inc. (Thomas Nelson Publishers, 1999), 135.

**53** Leon Morris, Pillar New Testament Commentary: the Gospel According to Matthew (Wm. B. Eerdman's Publishing Co., 1992), 187-190.

**54** Stanley N. Gundry, Love Them In: The Life and Theology of D. L. Moody (Moody Press, 1999), 53-54, 152-153, 171-172.

**55** F. Brown, S. Driver, C. Briggs, The Brown-Driver-Briggs Hebrew and English Lexicon (Hendrickson Publishers, 1996), 829c.

**56** Bauer, Danker, Arndt, and Gingrich, A Greek-English Lexicon of the New Testament and other Christian Literature (The University of Chicago Press, 2000), katallage, 521.

**57** "A Science Odyssey: People and Discoveries" (PBS, 1998). http://www.pbs.org/wgbh/aso/databank/entries/dm52sa.html. Retrieved 2012-03-26.

**58** David F. Wells, The Courage to Be Protestant (Wm. Eerdmans Publishing Co., 2008), 132-133.

# APPENDIX B:
## SCRIPTURE INDEX

# ROM

# APPENDIX C:
## SUBJECT INDEX

For more information about

# MICHAEL E. LOOMIS

&

# 10 LEPERS

please visit:

*facebook.com/10.Lepers*

*mloomis530209@gmail.com*

- - - - - - - - - - - - - -

For more information about
AMBASSADOR INTERNATIONAL
please visit:

*www.ambassador-international.com*
*@AmbassadorIntl*
*www.facebook.com/AmbassadorIntl*

www.ingramcontent.com/pod-product-compliance
Lightning Source LLC
Chambersburg PA
CBHW061825040426
42447CB00012B/2827